Leading the Lawmakers
Sam Rayburn

Britannica Bookshelf—Great Lives

Leading the Lawmakers

SAM RAYBURN

by Edward Allen

ENCYCLOPAEDIA BRITANNICA PRESS

Chicago   New York   London

This book is for John Nance Garner,
former Vice President of the United States.
Mr. Sam would agree.

TABLE OF CONTENTS

Chapter 1

"Be a Man"

Congressman Joseph Weldon Bailey had selected a Saturday morning for an important speech in Bonham, Texas, to the voters of his district. Now that the day was here he was a little concerned, for it was rainy. Bonham was a small town, and the success of Bailey's speech depended on his reaching not just the "city folk" but those who lived in the country as well.

He needn't have been worried, for when he arrived at the large tent that also served as one of Bonham's churches, he found it full. The country people had come into town to hear the man who was representing them in Washington, D. C.

One of those in the crowd was a boy of 12 or 13, just beginning to be interested in such things as what Congressmen have to say. He had finished his farm chores early that Saturday, washed off his feet at the pump, and climbed on a mule for the ride into Bonham over several miles of muddy road. When he came to the big tent, he hesitated. Inside, the place was jammed with people, many of them from Bonham itself. The boy looked at their clothes and then at his own. Embarrassed, he decided to stay outside in the rain. He walked around the tent until he finally found an opening through which he could see and hear without actually going inside.

Fascinated, the boy—young Samuel Taliaferro Rayburn—listened to Bailey as he spoke for a full two hours. When he had finished, Sam slipped around to the front of the tent again and waited for Representative Bailey to come out. He was a tall, handsome man, and as he strode by, he towered over stocky young Sam. Sam followed him for five or six blocks through the streets of Bonham until the Congressman climbed aboard a streetcar, leaving Sam watching and thinking with the soft rain still falling on his bare head. He turned away slowly, the image of Bailey still huge in his mind, and he wondered if he could ever be as big a man as the great Joe Bailey.

At this moment, the course of young Sam Rayburn's life was decided. He would become a speaker like Joe Bailey—and he would sit in the faraway halls of the Congress of the United States! Sam Rayburn walked with a new purpose as he returned to the mule that had carried him to Bonham from his home in Flag Springs, south of town. Quickly he swung onto the animal's back and headed home.

As soon as he got home, Sam announced his plans to become a Congressman like Joe Bailey. His father and mother listened carefully, for they knew their son was serious about his new ambition. Sam stood by the fire in his family's small country home, talking with his parents and feeling his new dream beginning to take strong roots in his mind. He told his brothers and sisters, too, and he spoke with such seriousness that they did not doubt for a minute that someday his ambition to be a Congressman would be fulfilled.

So, on a rainy Saturday in a small town of the great North Texas prairie, the United States unknowingly received the prom-

[10]

ise of one of the most devoted statesmen in its history. The name of Sam Rayburn was destined to become one of the most loved and respected in the House of Representatives in Washington, D. C. His career as Congressman from the Fourth District of Texas was to extend without interruption from 1913 until 1961. Twenty-five consecutive times, the voters of the Fourth District would elect Rayburn and send him to Washington. Eight presidents would dwell in the White House while Rayburn served in the Congress. Each came to know Rayburn well, because from his earliest days in Washington, he was one of the House's most active and important members. And from 1940 on, when he was first elected to the historic office of Speaker of the House of Representatives, Sam Rayburn was continuously regarded as the most important man in the legislative branch of the government of the United States.

That such a man as Sam Rayburn should come from a farmhouse on the North Texas prairie to the heights of leadership of Congress is not an unusual event in American history. Rayburn was even born in a log cabin, the symbol that has long been associated with the opportunity all Americans have to rise from poverty into greatness. Sam Rayburn was born on January 6, 1882, on a small farm near Lenoir, Tennessee, in the log cabin his father had built a few years earlier.

William Marion Rayburn, young Sam's father, was a native of the rocky hills of East Tennessee; and he fought through the Civil War with the great Confederate general, Nathan Bedford Forrest. After the war was over, Marion Rayburn married Martha Waller in 1868. Martha was something of an aristocrat in the Tennessee hills, for she could trace her family back to the time when William the Conquerer took England in 1066. With Marion Rayburn, whose education was too brief for him even to learn to read and write, Martha made an interesting contrast. Around the cozy fire in their Tennessee home, Marion told the Rayburn children of his experiences with Forrest's cavalry during the war, and Martha Rayburn read to them from their small library.

By 1887, Marion and Martha Rayburn had ten children in their log home in Tennessee—two of them younger than Sam. The Civil War had left deep scars on their part of the country, and the opportunity for getting ahead around Lenoir was getting worse with each year. Marion worked the small farm, raising corn as his principal crop and planting enough other vegetables to feed his large family. It was a bare and tough life. Marion began thinking more and more of moving away from his beloved Tennessee to a newer, fresher country that might offer his family more in return for his long hours of farm work. The answer, he decided at last, was 1,000 miles away in Texas.

Marion Rayburn discussed his decision with his wife, and she agreed that they should leave the farm near Lenoir and move to the fertile blackland prairie of north Texas. Young Sam, along with his brothers and sisters, scrambled into the wagon and the Rayburn family went to Lenoir, where they caught a train to take them on the first leg of the long journey. From the train window, five-year-old Sam watched other families who were also making the great move to the West, the men dressed in plainsmen's clothes with wide-brimmed hats and carrying rifles slung across their shoulders. The people moved in great caravans of covered wagons, following the certain path of the railroad to the West—and young Sam Rayburn watched with fascination and excitement.

The Rayburn family arrived in Dodd City in the eastern part of Fannin County, Texas, on the Texas and Pacific railroad. For a short while they stayed with some relatives who had already moved to Fannin County, but Marion Rayburn was eager to have a home of his own as soon as possible. In November of 1887, he bought a 40 acre farm south of the little town of Windom. In 1890, and again in 1897, he bought more land in the same area, now known as Flag Springs. Sam Rayburn called this part of Fannin County and the nearby county seat of Bonham home for the rest of his life.

His education began at Burnett, about 12 miles south of Bonham, and several miles from the Rayburn home at Flag Springs. But the following year, 1891, Sam transferred to the new school at Flag Springs. The walk was much shorter for Sam, but the new school was far removed from our present idea of what new schools are like. There were no chairs or desks in the one-room building. All the students sat at long benches, with about 12 students at each bench. Sam was remembered by his teachers as a good student who always knew his lessons. He was especially good at "spelling bees," and was usually the winner or one of the last ones to get "spelled down."

Along with his school work and the chores he had to do around the farm, Sam still found time to play with the other boys who attended the Flag Springs school. In addition to two favorite swimming holes, there was rabbit hunting in the winter and baseball in the summer. Sam played in the outfield, while two of his brothers, Dick and Tom, were pitchers. His love for baseball continued throughout his career as a Congressman in Washington. He was a frequent visitor to the games of the Washington Senators and for several years played in the annual game between the Democrats and Republicans in the House of Representatives.

In all, Sam's was a happy life in the 1890's. Working with his father on the farm kept him and all his brothers busy, but it produced more happiness than the rocky little place in Tennessee could ever have done. Then, when young Sam heard Congressman Bailey's two-hour speech in Bonham, the years of hard work and hard study at school began to make sense. He continued until his course was completed in the grammar school at Flag Springs; then he spent all his time helping his father on the farm. He was 17 years old.

As he worked, he thought more and more about his ambition to some day follow in the footsteps of Congressman Joe Bailey. And as he helped Marion Rayburn plow the rich blackland fields and make the spring planting for the year's cotton crop, he realized his work on the farm was not helping him reach his important goal.

The days stretched on, and young Sam knew he would have to make a decision soon or forget the whole idea and what he wanted to do with his life. Finally, when it came to just that, there could only be one answer. He stopped his work in the cotton field and told his father he wanted to talk with him about something very important.

Marion Rayburn listened carefully as his son told him he wanted to go away to college. Sam did not ask his father for any money at all, explaining that he was sure he could take care of his own expenses. In fact, Sam told his father there would be no problem in getting the cotton picked that summer and that the only thing he wanted was his father's approval for him to go.

Perhaps Marion Rayburn would have preferred for Sam to stay with him on the farm at Flag Springs. But he knew Sam's mind had been made up for several years—and he knew very well, indeed, that when a Rayburn's mind is decided, more talking is unnecessary. He gave his consent, but he reminded his son there was absolutely no extra money to give him and that he would have to earn his own way through college. The only thing, Marion Rayburn told his son, he could give was character. But what more could any son ask? Certainly, it proved to be a wonderful gift for Sam Rayburn.

So the future was decided. In the fall of that year, 1900, after the cotton was picked, Sam Rayburn packed his few possessions into a tight bundle and tied them with a short piece of rope. He said good-bye to his mother at their home, and his father drove him into the little town of Ladonia in the southeastern corner of Fannin County. They made the trip in a buggy over poor roads and it took several hours, even though the distance from Flag Springs was only a few miles. When they arrived in Ladonia, Sam's father bought the train ticket. Then he did a surprising thing. Slowly, he reached deep into his pocket and pulled out several crumpled bills. Counted out into Sam's hand, they came to $25. Sam knew it was all the money his father had.

Father and son stood together quietly on the platform then, waiting for the train that would carry Sam to Mayo College in Commerce, Texas. When it came, Marion Rayburn took his son's hand firmly and spoke one brief sentence to him that would ring forever in Sam Rayburn's mind:

"Sam," he said, "be a man!"

With this, the two parted. One, the old Confederate soldier, who had given his son the richest and the greatest gifts he knew. The other, a determined young man who had taken these gifts of character and of strength and was beginning his journey. It was destined to carry him farther than either of them ever dreamed would be possible.

Chapter 2

Going into Politics

Sam Rayburn climbed aboard the train and it pulled slowly away. He rode it only a few miles to Wolfe City in nearby Hunt County, just to the south. There, he caught the train to Commerce and Mayo College. The distance of the trip from his home in Flag Springs was only 14 miles as the crow flies. The great difficulty in travelling through Texas at the turn of the century is highlighted by Sam's long ride to get 14 miles from home!

As 17-year-old Sam Rayburn rode, he watched the slowly passing countryside of his part of the huge state of Texas, known as the Fourth Congressional District. It is a country of easy rolling, low green hills that blend into one another and leave a general impression of almost flatness. Lying in the great middle portion of the state, the Fourth District is not so heavily wooded as the pine country of the deep East Texas forests. And it is not like the barren and dry land that stretches away to the west until it finally lifts up into the tall Texas mountains beyond the Pecos River. The Fourth District is a softer country than

[16]

that to the west, but tougher than the wooded sweet hills to the east. All of these parts of Texas—and the coastline along the Gulf of Mexico and the beautiful Hill Country of Austin and San Antonio, Sam Rayburn would one day know well. But for now, Texas to him was this simple prairie of low hills he saw from the window of the train.

Already, Sam had begun to think about this wide country and what he might one day do to make it better. His politics were decided: with his heritage of association with the embattled Southern states, he came quite naturally into the fold of the Democratic party, with its promise of equality for the defeated states in the Confederacy. But more important was young Sam's hard belief in an honest government whose purpose was to serve its people in the best possible way. As he rode along on the final leg of his trip to Commerce, the beginnings of some of the country's best laws were taking shape in Sam's mind.

When the train arrived in Commerce, Sam got off, still holding his bundle of clothes under his arm. The town seemed so strange to Sam that it could well have been on the other side of the world! He reached into his pocket and felt the comfort of the $25 his father had given him. Then he turned and began walking toward the campus of Mayo College.

Later, Mayo College became East Texas State College, and it has now taken its place as one of the state's best colleges. But in Sam's college days, it offered a limited course of study and had very few students. Mayo College reflected completely the personality of its founder: William Leonidas Mayo. The motto of the college was "Ceaseless Industry, Fearless Investigation, and Unfettered Thought." And since Professor Mayo was the proprietor, he saw to it that his motto was carried out by every student there. In all, it was a happy environment for Sam.

Even Sam's shaky financial condition did not present a severe problem, for most of Mayo's students were poor. Professor Mayo gave Sam the job as bell ringer for the school, and he picked up an additional $6 a month working as a janitor and helping one of the local men with his chores at milking time. With his room and board costing only $8 a month, he was just able to get by without dipping too far into his $25.

But it wasn't easy. Many times during his first year at Mayo, Sam would pull the shades down over his dormitory window and get out his washboard and tub to do his own laundry. In this way, Sam made his money go a little further and found a way to do some of the things he wanted to do. For one thing, Sam enjoyed buying the books he really liked for his permanent collection. He bought such volumes as Philip Gilbert Hamerton's *Intellectual Life* and *Outlines of English History* and Ralph Waldo Emerson's *Representative Men*.

On the lighter side, Sam's first year at Mayo was much the same as college freshmen experience today. On one occasion, Sam and a friend borrowed a surrey—complete with a square top and fringe—to take their girl friends for a Sunday afternoon drive in the country out from Commerce. As they rode along, one of the girls spotted a peach orchard and hinted for the boys to pick a few for them. Sam, of course, was eager to please the young ladies, and he pulled the horse to a halt. The boys climbed over the fence and into the peach orchard. Then, just as they were about to begin picking the best of the peaches, the owner of the orchard, who had been watching silently all the while, set loose his dogs.

Surprised, Sam and his friend turned away quickly from the delicious looking fruit and began running for their surrey. The dogs were barking fiercely and closing in on them fast as Sam's friend scrambled over the top rail of the fence. Sam, however, was not quite so fortunate. For just as Sam reached the top rail, one of the dogs reached Sam. He pulled away and climbed on over the fence, but left behind in the angry dog's jaws was the seat of Sam's pants. The rest of the afternoon Sam was very careful to face the two young ladies at all times.

Such was Sam Rayburn's life in his first year of college: serious study, hard work, and a liberal sprinkling of old-fashioned fun. But at the end of the first year, Sam's money was gone, and he was not earning enough to pay his full expenses at Mayo. Unhappily, he realized he could not continue during the coming year. But he had qualified for a teacher's certificate, and he decided to spend one year teaching, save his money, and then return to Mayo for his bachelor's degree. He received an assignment to teach in Greenwood, which was only a few

Sam Rayburn at 21

THE SAM RAYBURN LIBRARY

miles from Commerce and his friends who were still attending Mayo. During 1901, he taught school and saved as much of his salary as he could. When he returned to the college, he had saved enough to stay until he was graduated in 1903.

During his final years at Mayo, Sam began to build quite a reputation as a speaker. He was the leader of the Oratorical Association with ten members on his team. And of course it pleased Sam a great deal when several of his friends in Commerce even suggested that he should go into politics.

But with graduation, there were more debts to pay, and Sam realized he was still a little young to consider running for public office. So he once again took a job as a school teacher, this time at Dial, Texas. He was there for two terms, from 1903 to 1905, and then moved to another teaching assignment at Lannius. Both towns were near the Rayburn home in Flag Springs, so he could spend a good deal of time with his family.

By 1906, all of Sam's debts from college were paid in full, and he even had small savings to show for his years of teaching. He was 24 years old now, and he knew the time had come to make another important move. Sam enjoyed his work in teaching and he loved the association with young students, but it was not, after all, getting him any nearer to the Congress of the United States. He made his decision and announced to the school board at Lannius that he would not be returning for the next semester. He explained that he had decided to run for Representative in the State Legislature at Austin, Texas.

Going into politics—even in 1906 in Fannin County— not only took courage and confidence. It also required money. Generally, there are two ways an aspiring politician can solve this problem: he can spend his own money on the campaign, if he has enough. Or he can have a lot of friends who are eager enough to see him elected that they will make the necessary contributions. Sam Rayburn solved it the second way, by necessity. With the backing he needed, Sam Rayburn set out for the first time to win the voters' confidence—and their votes.

Somewhat differently from many states, Rayburn's campaign was fought in the hot months of the Texas summer. The Terrell Election Law of 1905 requires that all candidates for state and national office must receive nomination of their political party in a primary, or first, election, held in July. So actually, Sam Rayburn was running for the Democratic Party's nomination as its candidate for the legislature. Of course, in Fannin County, there were very few Republicans and winning the Democratic primary was assurance of election in November.

So it was in the heat of the summer sun that Sam Rayburn mounted a brown pony and began to visit with the voters of Fannin County. He travelled all the roads in the county, stopping to visit with each farmer. He discussed cotton, cattle, corn, hogs—and farm problems in general with them. Having lived and worked for years with his father, it was not a difficult task for the young politician to convince the voters that he was, in truth, one of them. And before he left to go on to the next farm, he displayed an early sign of his instinct for successful campaigning. He asked the man with whom he had been talking for the name of his neighbor. In this way, Rayburn could always greet the next man by name. It is this sort of touch that wins votes.

Later in the campaign, Rayburn and his opponent, Sam Gardner, campaigned together, making their way over Fannin County's dusty roads in a one-horse buggy. When they came to a small community, they waited for a crowd to gather around them. Then they would take turns speaking to the group. Toward the end of Rayburn's and Gardner's race for the Legislature, Gardner became too ill to travel and speak. Rather than seize an unfair advantage, Sam helped take care of his opponent for several days until they could resume their trips and talks.

Finally, the campaign was over. The election was held on a Saturday, and Sam Rayburn returned to his home in Flag Springs to wait for the outcome. It was the following Tuesday before all the votes were counted in Bonham and the results were announced: Sam Rayburn had won his first political race by 163 votes over Sam Gardner!

When the celebration in the Rayburn home had subsided, the family realized that another farewell would have to be said to Sam.

It was an entirely different Sam Rayburn who was leaving his home in Flag Springs than it had been in 1900 when he left for Mayo College. At 24, the young legislator had the mark of a mature, professional man. Even his thinning hair gave him an older and wiser appearance than most men his age. His family and his friends saw him off with their affection and best wishes.

Chapter 3

Stepping Stones

M ost of young legislator Sam Rayburn's first term in Austin was spent "learning the ropes." This is the natural pattern of development for a new Representative in the State Legislature, and Sam Rayburn followed the pattern as well as he could. "Freshmen" Representatives in Austin knew they were to be seen and not heard until they had gained experience.

It was not an easy task, however, for the Representative from Fannin County; for his earlier idol, now United States Senator Joseph Weldon Bailey, was under severe fire throughout the early months of 1907. Rumors were flying about that Senator Bailey had undesirable connections with both the Standard Oil Company and several large railroads. In those days U. S. Senators were elected by State Legislatures. In Texas, at that time, any suggestion that a politician was working for "Big Business" was considered almost a criminal accusation. So when Sam Rayburn heard the rumors and saw the Legislature organizing an investigation, even threatening the Senator with removal from office, he ignored the possibility that Senator Bailey might have done anything wrong. This was a Rayburn trademark, even when he was only 25 years old.

During the Thirtieth Legislature, the other main point of interest was the old Texas question of prohibition. Rayburn himself—even in those early days of his political career—had no personal inclination to either the "wets" or the "drys." By birth, he was naturally cast in the camp of the "drys," who were opposed to the sale of alcoholic beverages. The young representative from Fannin County, however, took the position that the people themselves should decide the question of whether liquor was to be sold in their area.

By the end of Sam's first term in the Legislature, such matters as the state's confusing liquor laws convinced him that he needed more education than his B.S. degree from Mayo College had provided. He enrolled in the University of Texas Law School in Austin. By 1908 he had taken and passed the state bar examination, which enabled him to practice law in Texas. Promptly, he opened his law office in Bonham, the county seat of Fannin County. Also, he announced his candidacy for election to a second term of office as Representative in the Texas House of Representatives. That summer, 1908, he again won the Democratic primary that would send him to the 31st Legislature in January, 1909.

When the Legislature convened, Representative Rayburn had served his years of apprenticeship. As a result, he received several important committee appointments from Speaker A. M. Kennedy. He was put on the Committee of Education, the Committee of Private Corporations, the extremely important Committee on Constitutional Amendments, and was made Chairman of the Committee on Banks and Banking. It was an impressive load for such a young member of the Legislature.

Soon after the 31st Legislature got under way, one of its members, Representative Gaines, brought some serious charges against Speaker Kennedy, accusing him of spending an excessive amount of state treasury money to furnish the Speaker's office in the Capitol.

Rayburn moved immediately to the Speaker's defense, for he knew the attack was merely a form of punishment for some act in the past that had offended Representative Gaines and the Administration. The Representative from Fannin County pointed out that Speaker Kennedy's purchases of furniture were to be used by future Speakers of the House as well as himself. And, Rayburn added, they were quite in line with the expenses for furniture in the state Senate, expenses that were not being criticized at all.

Despite the good sense of Rayburn's arguments in Kennedy's behalf, the House voted a resolution that required Kennedy to pay the state $120 and make a formal apology to the House of Representatives. Quite naturally, Speaker Kennedy offered his resignation.

Then, according to the tradition, gifts were presented to the retiring Speaker in a session of the House. The pages, clerks, stenographers, and the full membership of the House each presented Kennedy with a parting gift—with each group designating one of the representatives as its spokesman. The Negro porters of the House asked Sam Rayburn to make their presentation of a beautiful chafing dish. Rayburn happily accepted and when his turn came to speak, he proceeded to steal the show from his fellow members. In summing up, he described the generosity of the Negro porters in 1909. ". . . man's soul," Rayburn said with quiet deliberation, "is not to be charged to the color of his skin. Though his skin be brown or black it is possible that it holds a soul as pure and spotless as any man's!"

[25]

The Legislature was quiet as it listened to the man from Fannin County. For here was one of their own—the son of a Confederate soldier—reminding them of the quality of mankind. It was one of his first public statements on a subject that was to become one of intense interest to the entire nation. Rayburn's fellow legislators in Austin listened as he spoke, and they could not disagree with anything the man from Fannin said.

Rayburn sat down, knowing his point was made. From then on, whenever he rose to speak on the floor of the State Legislature, other members paid attention. Sam Rayburn always spoke in simple, direct language that cut through to the very soul of his subject.

THE SAM RAYBURN LIBRARY

Standing before the Rayburn home at Flag Springs (left to right), Sam's parents, Uncle Jim, brothers Abner and Dick, Sam, and sister Lucinda

At home in Flag Springs, Marion and Martha Rayburn followed their son's activities with great joy. In February of 1909, Sam's mother wrote, "We are proud of the record you are making. Hope you will march onward and upward." And later, in March of the same year: ". . . Also glad you are always present [when the House meets] and on the side that we think is right."

Such was the career of Sam Rayburn in the 31st Legislature. His reputation throughout Fannin County was exceeded only by the growing respect his work in Austin created in the House. In the spring of 1910, the decision to run for a third term in the Legislature was easy to make, even though Fannin County had never elected a state representative to a third term. But that July, Rayburn broke the tradition and swept to victory.

Another winner in the primary was O. B. Colquitt, who was elected the next governor of Texas over three other candidates. In the months that followed, Colquitt began to formulate his program of the laws he wanted to be passed by the 32nd Legislature. As always, the governor was particularly interested in whom the House of Representatives would elect as Speaker. Colquitt naturally wanted to have a Speaker in the House who would help him get his program through the legislative branch of the state government. And among those Representatives who announced their candidacy was Rayburn.

But Sam Rayburn was not the new Governor's choice for Speaker. First of all, Governor Colquitt was a "wet" and was opposed to having any area in the state that did not allow the sale of liquor. Rayburn's position was that each area should be allowed to make its own decision in the matter. The second reason Colquitt did not want Rayburn for Speaker was his desire to have a man who was strongly opposed to U. S. Senator Joe Bailey. Jeff Cox met these requirements; Rayburn did not.

Samuel Taliaferro Rayburn in the Texas Legislature

Just before the 32nd Legislature opened, the man who seemed most likely to win as Speaker was still another than Cox, C. E. Gilmore. This candidate for the office had strong backing from the "drys" on the liquor question and from many Joe Bailey supporters. Even so, no one was counting the man from Fannin out of the race. His moderate position on the liquor question appealed to both the "wets" and the "drys." Perhaps even more important was the individual who was working hard at his side, former Speaker A. M. Kennedy, whom Sam Rayburn had helped in earlier days. Too, there was the advantage of Rayburn's immense popularity.

On January 9, 1911, the day before the opening session of the Legislature, Governor Colquitt's favorite, Jeff Cox, was obviously in trouble. Colquitt's control of the Legislature was not strong enough to push Cox through to victory. That night, Cox issued a statement withdrawing from the race.

The two principal contenders left were Gilmore and Rayburn. The "wets" preferred Rayburn for his moderate view of the liquor question. Gilmore without a doubt had the vote of the "drys." Meanwhile, in a brilliant political move, Kennedy had been using his friendship with Senator Joe Bailey. Many of Bailey's supporters switched from Cox or Gilmore to the man from Fannin County. When Cox withdrew from the race on the night before the election for Speaker, many felt that Kennedy had successfully obtained Bailey's support for Sam Rayburn. In a matter of a few days, Rayburn moved from being a dark horse to a position as the favorite candidate.

The next day, January 10, the Legislature convened. Early in the official business of its first day was the election of a Speaker. Only the two were nominated, Gilmore and Rayburn. When the vote was taken, an error was discovered and the vote had to be repeated. The final count was: Rayburn, 70 votes; Gilmore, 63. At 29 years of age, Sam Rayburn was Speaker of the 32nd Legislature. With the announcement, Rayburn let out a loud yell and jumped to his feet for joy. Then, a little embarrassed, he sat down again as his friends and supporters pressed around him to offer their congratulations.

A few moments later, the new Speaker was escorted to the rostrum to receive the oath of office. Rayburn's acceptance speech was short: "The members of this House have just paid me a compliment I do not fail to appreciate. This office carries with it duties and responsibilities which I do not fail to appreciate. The loyalty of the friends who have stood by me in this campaign is such that a life of friendship is too short to repay them. I hope to preside over this House to its satisfaction and the glory of this great commonwealth. I would not be true to myself nor my friends if I did not thank this House on this occasion not only for myself, but for every friend. But up there in Fannin County, there is an old man already passed his three-score and there by his side sits an old woman at whose feet I would now delight to worship. For them, I also thank you."

In concluding, the new Speaker of the Texas House said, "There is no feeling of bitterness by me for those who have opposed me in this campaign. The man who was pitted against me is a gentleman in every sense of the word." For Sam Rayburn, this was a typical attitude. He respected and was often very friendly with those who opposed him.

During the 32nd Texas Legislature, the Rayburn-led House of Representatives passed important legislation that controlled child labor and provided shorter working hours for women in the state. Also, the establishment of a Confederate Veterans Women's home and a tuberculosis sanitarium were approved. It was, altogether, a successful year. When the session was finished, a resolution was presented to the young Speaker giving him the House's thanks for the "fairness and intelligent manner with which he has presided over the desk as Speaker of the House . . . . we congratulate the people of Texas on having had the services of Mr. Rayburn. . . ."

Several of the gifts that the House presented to its Speaker indicated knowledge of Rayburn's intention to keep moving up the political ladder. One was a traveling bag presented by the porters; another was a suitcase from the young pages of the House. Rayburn's good friend, A. M. Kennedy, presented a gold watch as a gift from the membership of the House and remarked seriously that he hoped it would keep good time for Sam in Washington.

Sam Rayburn accepted the gifts but gave no indication of his plans. Meanwhile, rumors flew throughout Austin that

[30]

the Speaker would make a bid for Congress in the 1912 campaign. But the office of Speaker in the Texas Legislature was usually a stepping-stone to a statewide race for either Governor or Attorney General. At the time, no one was certain of Sam Rayburn's political plans.

The people waited for him to announce his decision.

Chapter 4

On to Washington

O n January 6, 1912, Sam Rayburn celebrated his 30th birthday. And his friends in Fannin County could see that three terms—six years—in the Texas Legislature had seasoned him. He stood now with a square set to his shoulders that eventually would be famous across the nation, wore his hat pulled hard over his piercing eyes, and kept his right hand pushed deep into his side coat pocket. Even then, at 30, the most famous Rayburn trademark of all, his bald head, was beginning to present itself through his seriously thinning hair.

As January drew to a close, Sam Rayburn had still not officially announced his plans. But the people were beginning to talk, sensing one of the hottest races for Congress in many years. The main reason for this feeling was State Senator B. B. Sturgeon of Lamar County, just to the east of Fannin. Sturgeon and Speaker Rayburn had maintained a spirited feud for months in Austin. When the session had ended, Sturgeon hinted strongly that he was preparing to run for Congress. At that time Lamar County was in the same Congressional district as Rayburn's. Both men commanded large followings in their home counties, and the people were eager for the official announcements to be made. But unfortunately, the Congressional districts of the state were changed in 1912 in a reapportionment based on the 1910 Census. Sturgeon's Lamar County and Rayburn's Fannin were placed in separate Congressional Districts.

On February 2, 1912, the man from Fannin County made his official announcement of candidacy for Congressman from the new Fourth District of Texas. But Sam Rayburn was not to be elected to Congress without a battle. Within a short time of his own announcement, no fewer than seven other citizens paid their filing fees and entered the race against him!

Rayburn began his campaign, but this time not on the back of a brown pony as he had when he first ran for the Legislature. He bought a Model-T Ford and began travelling the country roads throughout the District. No longer would it be enough to campaign only in Fannin County. Now Rayburn had to reach more than 200,000 people in five Texas counties and convince them they should send him to Washington.

In a major speech at Bonham, with the district courtroom filled to capacity, Sam Rayburn put forward his belief:

"I," he said in a dramatic opening, "am a Democrat." The applause thundered through the room. Rayburn's speech lasted two hours and the people listened intently, just as they had listened to Congressman Joseph Weldon Bailey many years before when Sam Rayburn himself was in the audience, peeking through a flap in the tent. Now it was Rayburn's hour.

Summing up his philosophy, he said: "I believe that the principles advocated and adhered to by the Party since its birth are the same fundamental principles upon which our

[33]

Republic was founded: a government of the people, by the people and for the people, where every man, rich or poor, should stand equal before the law and Government with . . . 'equal rights to all and special privileges to none.' This is the Democratic doctrine. . . ."

Then, in a typical stroke of Rayburn humor and smart politics, he said, "I will not deny that there are men in the District better qualified than I to go to Congress." Rayburn paused. "But, gentlemen, *these men are not in the race!*"

During his campaign for membership in the United States Congress, Sam Rayburn touched on the important questions of the day. In national politics, he argued that the Republicans' 16 years had been too long a tenure in the White House. He opposed placing a high, protective tariff on goods from foreign countries. Since the farmer who produces the raw materials was not protected, why should the manufacturer be? Rayburn stated that he would like to see completely free trade.

The federal income tax was not yet a law in 1912. The man from Fannin County said in his campaign that the wealthy —rather than the poor—should bear the heavier part of the tax load. Then—in a political left hook at the Republican party— he expressed himself as favoring a federal inheritance tax. He pointed out that the government could derive a great deal of revenue from fortunes built by tariff protected manufacturers.

As the campaign came into its final weeks, Rayburn's opponents realized he was pulling away from the pack. Desperately, they tried the well-known political tactic of mudslinging—telling the voters that Rayburn had special interests in the Santa Fe Railroad because his law partners in Bonham were attorneys for the corporation. Just as with the earlier accusation aimed at Joe Bailey, this was a serious political charge. Rayburn, however, answered the accusation well. He

[34]

explained that his partners did offer him part of the railroad's fee, but that he had refused it. He explained that as a member of the Legislature he had been representing the people of Fannin County and that his experience had taught him that representatives should not be close to corporations whose activities might someday become the subject of legislation.

Rayburn's views on labor were destined to make both friends and enemies. He contended that labor clearly had the right to organize in unions and that labor should be protected by law from unfair practices by management. But, he added, management had rights that must receive equal protection.

Election day arrived, July 27, 1912, and 21,336 votes were cast in the Fourth District of Texas. Of the seven candidates in the Democratic primary, Sam Rayburn won by a margin of 490 votes. Rayburn received 4,983 votes, while Tom Perkins received 4,493. Others in the race gathered from 4,365 to as low as 290 votes. It was not an overwhelming victory, but with seven other candidates in the race it was clearly an important win for the man from Fannin. His victory in July meant election for Sam Rayburn to his boyhood ambition: membership in the United States House of Representatives.

Sam Rayburn's public statement of his appreciation to the people for electing him their Congressman appeared in all the newspapers of the Fourth District. He said that his "main hope" was to conduct the affairs of the office well enough that his supporters would have no cause to regret having voted for him. To his opponents and their supporters, he wrote in typical Rayburn fashion: "For the men who were opponents of mine in the race I have nothing but the very kindest feelings, and the only pang that comes to me in the hour of my triumph is that so many good men must suffer defeat. To those who supported my opponents I have no word of censure but shall strive to so

[35]

discharge the duties of the position that they will be led to believe that the people made no mistake in electing me."

Later in the year, Sam Rayburn was not the only Democrat who looked forward to life in Washington, D. C. For Woodrow Wilson had been swept to victory in the Presidential election by a split in the Republican opposition. While William Howard Taft and Theodore Roosevelt split the Republican vote, Wilson won the election, the first Democrat to come to the White House since Grover Cleveland in 1893: Wilson, with 435 electoral votes to Roosevelt's 88 and Taft's 8, had won a great victory for the victory-starved Democrats.

In Congress, too, Democratic victories gave the party control of both the House of Representatives and the Senate. In an atmosphere of happy confidence, the Fourth District's new Congressman planned to enter the forthcoming 63rd Congress of the United States. Happily, the new Congressman boarded the train on February 27, 1913, at Bells, Texas, a few miles west of Bonham. The inauguration of President-elect Woodrow Wilson was to be held on March 4, and Rayburn wanted to have time to look around Washington before the great event.

But before Rayburn arrived in the nation's capital, he made what some have felt was a major decision. All his life, he had used his middle name, Taliaferro, which is pronounced "Toliver." It made a long and somewhat awkward name for a man of Rayburn's crisp, direct personality. He decided it just didn't fit. So, Samuel Taliaferro Rayburn became simply Sam Rayburn of Texas.

Sam Rayburn of Texas arrived in Washington to begin his first of 25 consecutive terms as the Representative of the Fourth District. The inauguration of Woodrow Wilson on March 4, 1913, provided an exciting start for his career. He listened intently as the new President made his inaugural address.

Rayburn listened with deep admiration for the former Princeton scholar who was now the President. Through the years, Rayburn never lost this feeling of respect for Wilson, both as a man and as a President. He was the first of eight men Rayburn would know in the White House. The two men were never really close, for just as it had been in his early days in Austin, a period of apprenticeship was necessary. A young, first-year Congressman spends more time listening to other Congressmen than talking with the President.

As the 63rd Congress began, Sam Rayburn was quickly making friends on Capitol Hill. Among the first—and certainly among the most important—was a fellow Texan, John Nance Garner, the Congressman from Uvalde. Known as "Cactus Jack," Garner was one of the shrewdest politicians Washington had ever seen. Garner soon discovered the same talents were to be found in Sam Rayburn.

Garner was originally from the same general part of Texas as Rayburn, even though he now served as the representative from Uvalde, hundreds of miles away from Bonham in southwest Texas. Originally, Garner's home had been in Red River County, about 70 miles east of Rayburn's home. But in Cactus Jack's youth he had felt the sting of defeat when he ran for public office. Hurt and possibly even a little angry over his rejection at the polls, Garner left the northeast Texas area and moved 400 miles away to Uvalde. Many of Garner's friends and relatives, however, remain in the strip of Texas counties running along the Red River.

An early effect of Rayburn's affiliation with Garner was the appointment of the new Congressman to the House Committee on Interstate and Foreign Commerce. It is unusual for a freshman member of the House to receive such an important committee assignment; but what Jack Garner wanted in the

House of Representatives, he had a remarkable ability to get. He met with the chairman of the committee and explained that Sam Rayburn was more experienced than the average first-year representative. Carefully, Cactus Jack pointed out that Rayburn's career in the Texas Legislature gave him about the same qualifications as if he had been governor of Texas!

Garner's influence on Sam Rayburn is difficult to calculate, for in many ways the two men were already similar in their attitudes and habits. Of course, Garner had been in the House of Representatives for ten years when Rayburn arrived. He was already one of the Democratic party's most powerful leaders when Rayburn arrived in Washington. It cannot be denied that Rayburn learned a great deal about politics from Garner.

In personal habits the new representative from Fannin already shared much in common with Garner, and this doubtless served as the springboard for their long friendship. They were both from the same area of Texas, a fact important at that time. Texas, with such a wide area, varied greatly in the customs of its people from north to south and from east to west. Both men also had a country background and perhaps felt uncomfortable when first they entered into the totally different environment of Washington. If this was true of Sam Rayburn, his older friend quickly helped him to feel at home. For Jack Garner remained the same throughout his long and impressive career in government. He avoided the endless rounds of Washington cocktail parties and other functions that might force him into wearing white tie and tails. Garner got along pretty well with this attitude, for he rose to become Speaker of the House of Representatives, then Vice President and even a strong candidate for the Democratic nomination for President. Without the influence of Cactus Jack Garner, Sam Rayburn might well have tried to remold his own personality to fit the social order of

Washington. But he knew this was not necessary, for he saw Garner had had remarkable success without changing at all.

Soon after the 63rd Congress got underway, Garner invited Rayburn to share his office with him in the House office building. Here the two men became even closer friends, and Rayburn became acquainted with Cactus Jack's famous way of "striking a blow for Liberty"—a liberal portion of good Bourbon whisky cut with a liberal dash of "branch water." It was served in Garner's office to his close friends in the Congress: an occasion of friendship and good fun but always with strong elements of dignity. As the years passed, striking a blow for Liberty with Jack Garner took on some of the quality of a ritual.

Another outgrowth of Garner's influence on the Congress was a room in the Capitol that came to be known as the "Board of Education." A conference room actually, it served as a meeting place similar to Garner's own office. Here, members of Congress gathered—oftentimes with the best minds of both the Democratic and Republican parties represented—but membership in the Board of Education was by invitation only. It provided an opportunity to discuss the important problems of the day without interruption. As a friend of Jack Garner, Rayburn was early invited to this well-known meeting place.

Meanwhile, President Wilson was busy organizing the program of legislation he would request from the Congress. Within a few weeks, he appeared at a joint session of the two houses of Congress—the first President since Thomas Jefferson to make the trip from the White House to Capitol Hill. In his address to the legislative branch of the government, Wilson urged Congress to pass new legislation to reduce the tariff and bring free trade between the United States and the rest of the world. There was, of course, violent opposition to a lower tariff from those who wished to continue protecting high prices for American manufactured goods. Sam Rayburn, however, was not one of these, for he felt lower prices for equipment would greatly benefit the farmers of the Fourth District and the country.

So keen was Rayburn's interest in the lowering of the tariff, that he decided to use it as the occasion of his "maiden" speech before the House of Representatives. On May 6, 1913, Sam Rayburn asked for recognition from the Speaker, breaking the tradition that a freshman Congressman usually does not try to enter into debate.

"Mr. Chairman," Rayburn said, "as a new Member of this great body I, of course, feel that I should have regard to some extent for the long-established custom of this House, which . . . demands that discussion of questions shall be left in the main to the more mature members . . . but on the other hand, I feel that as a representative and commissioned spokesman of more than 200,000 citizens of the Fourth Congressional District of Texas I should be allowed to break . . . whatever of this custom remains, and exercise my constitutional right to speak my sentiments. . . ." The man from Fannin County then proceeded to point out some of the faults of the tariff laws that had been passed by the Republicans of earlier Congresses. As an example, he explained that the tariff law provided for protection of manufacturers of shoes from foreign competition. At the same time, Rayburn said, the hides from which shoes are made were on the free list and were unprotected by the tariff. This, Rayburn insisted, was unfair to the American consumer of manufactured shoes.

Going further, Rayburn explained that he felt that the only good purpose a tariff served was to raise money for the expenses of the government when it could not be done in some other way. A tax, Rayburn said, on inherited wealth would

[40]

provide the income lost by a lower tariff. "When a man by inheritance comes into a large fortune out of no effort on his own part and only by accident of birth . . . I believe he should be willing to pay some of it as a tribute to the [government] that protected his ancestry in the accumulation [of their wealth]," Rayburn said.

In closing his maiden speech before the House of Representatives, Sam Rayburn's strong voice filled the huge room as he explained some of his more general views on government: "I have always dreamed of a country which I believe this should be . . . one in which the citizenship is an educated and patriotic people, not swayed by passion and prejudice, and a country that shall know no East, no West, no North, no South, but [be] inhabited by a people liberty loving, patriotic, happy and prosperous. . . ." The man from Fannin sat down and his fellow Congresmen had received the first hint that Sam Rayburn, representing the people of the Fourth District of Texas, was also representing the people of the entire nation.

With the end of debate on the tariff question, Wilson's request was granted by Congress in the form of the Underwood-Simmons Tariff Act of 1913. Throughout, it received the complete support of Sam Rayburn.

But tariff reform was not Rayburn's only interest during his first term in the House. He turned immediately to another bill he had been working on for some time, a bill he personally wrote and presented to the House for action. He called it the Stock and Bond bill. Its purpose was to regulate the activity of railroads in the nation, especially in the way large stockholders of one railroad were often involved in the ownership of several others. Rayburn felt this overlapping ownership should not be allowed, and he proposed that regulations should be placed on railroads to assure their not making unreasonable profit.

[41]

Rayburn's bill passed the House of Representatives by an overwhelming vote of 325 to 12, but in the Senate, the bill ran into strong opposition and was defeated. Thus it did not go to President Wilson's desk to be signed into law. Even so, Wilson watched its progress through the House with interest. After the measure was voted down he wrote a short note:

"My Dear Mr. Rayburn: We have all looked on with admiration and genuine appreciation as your Stock and Bond bill has been put through the House. It seems to me you deserve a great deal of praise for your part in the matter, and I want to make my humble contribution to the congratulations which I am sure you must be receiving. Cordially and sincerely yours, Woodrow Wilson."

For a first-year member of Congress to get a congratulatory letter from the President was an outstanding accomplishment. In his first term, Sam Rayburn established himself as a respected member of the House of Representatives. And, as 1914 arrived, he looked forward eagerly to the months and years ahead. But he also knew that membership in the House was only good for two years, that with each new Congress every member must stand for election in his district. As spring came, he also knew Tom Perkins would run against him.

Tom Perkins had placed second in the 1912 campaign that Rayburn had won by the slim margin of 490 votes. The remaining 11,000 votes cast had been split among the other six candidates in the race. Thus Perkins believed he had an excellent chance of winning Sam Rayburn's place in Congress. Vigorously, Perkins began his campaign, attacking the man from Fannin on every count he could think of. Meanwhile, the 63rd Congress was still in session in Washington, and Rayburn could not leave to defend himself in the Fourth District. Later, he did manage to return for a few speeches, but his attention was drawn away by the illness and death of one of his brothers and by his concern for the activities still going on in Washington. Even Rayburn's closest friends began to be worried about the race, for Perkins was campaigning hard.

Finally, on July 25, the people of the Fourth District told Sam Rayburn how they felt about him. This time the man from Fannin beat Tom Perkins by almost 10,000 votes!

During the same month—July, 1914—the Rayburn family moved from its home in Flag Springs to a 120-acre farm just outside the city limits of Bonham. It was a major move for the family and it proved to be a permanent one. Sam immediately

THE SAM RAYBURN LIBRARY

The Rayburn home at Bonham, Sam and Lucinda on the steps

[43]

spent $2,500 on improvements for the farm and its house. Aside from an apartment he kept in Washington, the big white colonial house near Bonham was Sam Rayburn's final home. It stands near U. S. Highway 80, which runs east and west through Bonham and roughly follows the Red River for several hundred miles across the state. The land is flat all around and the Rayburn home can be seen for several miles by people driving into Bonham from the west.

But more important to Sam Rayburn, he could see several miles from its wide porch, several miles of the Fourth District he loved so well. He was always happiest when he was there, in the big house that has for many years been a landmark of the Texas scene.

Chapter 5

In the Minority

In 1915, the 64th Congress met. As Rayburn resumed work in the House, his thoughts turned first of all to trying again to get his Stock and Bond bill passed into law.

Rayburn even went so far as to discuss it with President Wilson at the White House. But the President was beginning to focus more and more of his attention on the worsening situation in Europe. World War I had begun in the summer of 1914. Wilson discouraged Congressman Rayburn, who left the interview disappointed but determined to see his bill passed.

President Wilson was right in concentrating on the new war in Europe, and Rayburn was simply not yet mature enough to understand Wilson's emphasis on the more urgent business of the nation. When the war started, Wilson had urged Americans not to become too involved by a distant "war with which we have nothing to do." In America, some people felt the Atlantic Ocean still separated the nation from whatever was going on in the rest of the world. This view is known as "isolationist," because it aims at isolating America from international affairs.

Even Wilson hoped this could be done to some extent, for in August of 1914 he had issued a proclamation of neutrality.

World War I involved two groups of nations, the Triple Entente of Great Britain, France, and Russia against the Central Powers of Germany and Austria-Hungary. In many ways it actually seemed the United States could maintain its neutral position. But strong historic ties, especially with England, could not be forgotten.

England tried to use its mighty navy to control the seas and thus cut off Germany from needed supplies. Still trying not to take either side, the United States mildly complained that Britain was in violation of international law. But the mild complaint was quickly offset by German submarine attacks on ships carrying American property and even American citizens.

In these early days of Rayburn's career as a lawmaker, his knowledge of foreign affairs was still developing. President Wilson was trying desperately to keep the nation at peace, and he spoke with hope that it could be done. Sam Rayburn took these statements from President Wilson as the final word. He believed the United States could maintain its neutrality.

But in May of 1915, Sam Rayburn, along with all Americans, received the shocking news that a German submarine had sunk the English ocean liner, *Lusitania*. The huge ship was sunk just off the coast of Ireland with the loss of 1,153 lives. And among the dead were 114 United States citizens. Anger at the vicious attack broke out in all sections of America, and even Sam Rayburn wondered how long the Atlantic Ocean could separate the country from war with Germany. Many citizens felt the sinking of the *Lusitania* was, in itself, justification for entering the war against the Central Powers. President Wilson decided, however, to keep the peace as long as he could. He demanded that Germany recognize America's neutral rights and restrict submarine warfare to prevent another *Lusitania* disaster. In September, 1915, the German ambassador agreed to Wilson's request.

But the German Navy did not stick by the agreement very long. The *Sussex* was sunk with two Americans on board and President Wilson sent an ultimatum to the German government, which replied with the Sussex Pledge in May of 1916, agreeing not to sink merchant ships without first saving human lives. For nine months, the Germans kept their promise.

Meanwhile, 1916 brought a revision of Rayburn's thoughts on military preparedness. He continued, along with President Wilson and many others, to hope and to believe the United States could stay out of the war. Rayburn and the nation turned their thoughts for the moment to the political problems of another election year.

As usual, Sam Rayburn was faced with a fight for his seat in the House of Representatives. This time, the opponent was Andrew Randell. Again, the man from Fannin County was forced to delay his campaign in the Fourth District. By the time he arrived, Randell was well on his way to convincing the voters that it was time for a change. Rayburn moved to the attack.

Randell was a "city boy" from nearby Sherman, one of the larger towns in the Fourth District. His father had served in Congress earlier, and young Andrew had lived all his life in Sherman and Washington until his father sent him to Princeton. This background was enough for Sam Rayburn to pounce on like a tiger in his talks to the farmers throughout the Fourth.

"Not an hour of toil," Rayburn exclaimed, "ever soiled his silken palms! . . ." And, "I worked 14 to 16 hours a day in the hot sun on a Fannin County farm, and I voted to make these white-handed, bay-windowed gentry work at least eight

[47]

hours a day under an electric fan. . . ." It was a withering blast from a master politician! The "city boy" didn't really stand a chance in a Congressional district comprised mostly of country people—and Sam Rayburn knew it. When the votes were counted, Rayburn had beaten his opponent and won his place in the House for two years more.

During the same summer, the Democrats and Republicans held their national conventions for the Presidential election in November. The Chief Justice of the Supreme Court, Charles Evans Hughes, won the nomination of the Republican Party while the Democrats nominated President Wilson for reelection. The Democrats' campaign slogan was "He Kept Us Out of War!" The Democrats knew they were in for a good fight. In 1912, Taft and Roosevelt had split the Republican vote. This time, the Republicans could get behind Hughes and put him into the White House if Wilson did only as well as in 1912, when he actually had not received a majority of the popular vote. But voters always hesitate to "change horses in the middle of the stream," and Wilson's campaign slogan made sense to the public. Once more, Wilson failed to get a majority of the popular vote. But it is the electoral vote that counts—and Wilson led Hughes by 23 votes in the Electoral College.

New problems arose in 1917. The German government announced that after January 31, it would not restrict its submarine warfare. A few weeks later, the British captured a note written by the German Foreign Secretary to the Mexican government. It suggested that an alliance with Germany would result in the return of Texas, New Mexico and Arizona to Mexico. This plan, no doubt, met with considerable objection from Sam Rayburn and John Garner!

The United States responded by breaking off diplomatic relations with the German government and immediately arming its merchant ships. By the end of February, the situation grew more tense and finally exploded as the German Navy attacked and sank four United States ships during March. Wilson's patience was at its end. On April 2, he called a special session of Congress and asked it to make a declaration of war between the United States and Germany. Congress did so on April 6.

The 65th Congress had just begun and it was faced with a mountain of legislation—most of it related to the war. It was a new experience for most of the lawmakers, including Sam Rayburn. Quickly the Congress passed the Selective Service Act drafting almost 3,000,000 men into the armed services. Next was the nationalization of the railroads, putting their management under the federal government.

Through all its work in 1917, Congress felt the strong presence of Sam Rayburn, now in his third term. He supported the necessary war-effort measures, but argued mildly when the nationalization of the railroads was being considered in the House. Rayburn recognized that control of transportation was desirable during World War I, but he felt a definite time should be set for returning the railroads to their owners. As presented, the bill made no promise of returning the railroads to their owners, even after the war. Rayburn pointed out the dangers in such a policy and that permanent government ownership of the railroads would be socialistic.

Rayburn's most important contribution during the war was the War Risk Insurance Act, which he wrote. It provided for insurance up to $10,000 for servicemen. The man from Fannin was close in spirit to the people he represented in Congress; and he appreciated the sacrifices each family was making in sending its sons to the war. Sam Rayburn's deep concern for such legislation as the War Risk Insurance Act was typical of

[49]

the humanitarian position he believed necessary in politics. Future amendments and extensions of his bill provided for veterans to receive education, hospitalization, and loans to purchase homes, farms or business property at low interest rates. More than any other man in Washington, Sam Rayburn of Texas was the father of what eventually during World War II became known as the G. I. Bill.

As 1918 began, there was more than 176,000 American troops in France. Meanwhile, President Wilson outlined in January his "Fourteen Points" program that was intended to bring a lasting peace to the world. But the war moved into its second year of American participation and the 65th Congress remained in session. With the spring, the Allies made final preparations for a summer fight—and Sam Rayburn received the unwanted news that a fight was on his own hands back home in the Fourth District. This time his opponent was from his own Fannin County, Richard Lovelace, and Rayburn was warned not to take him lightly. But there were pressing matters in Washington with the country still at war, and Rayburn felt his first duty was to stay on the job in Congress. Even though it might mean defeat, Rayburn decided not to make his usually thorough campaign in the Fourth District. He put in one brief appearance, then quickly returned to Washington. When the primary vote was in, Rayburn had won his fourth term in Congress.

The Allied attack began in the summer, and by the fall, the enemy's back was broken. Finally, in November, all resistance to the Allies collapsed and a temporary German government made its plea for an armistice. On November 11, 1918, the fighting ended.

In the Congressional elections of 1918, the people of the United States swept the Republican party back into partial power, giving them control of both the Senate and the House of Representatives. For the first time since his election to Congress in 1912, Sam Rayburn found himself a member of the minority party. The change of power in Congress was not, however, entirely unexpected. In Wilson's campaign for reelection in 1916, Republican Hughes actually had received a majority of the popular vote.

The Republicans were joyful as the 66th Congress opened in 1919. With their majority, the Republicans elected a new Speaker of the House, Frederick H. Gillett of Massachusetts. With all the enthusiasm of political victors, the Republicans looked forward to the years ahead.

The Democrats, on the other hand, felt despair as the power of Congress slipped away from them. Champ Clark, who had nearly won the Democratic nomination for President in 1912, stepped down as Speaker of the House, a position he had held since 1911. The leadership of the Democratic party was compelled to adjust to a minority role.

Just as the Democrats were weakened in Congress, President Wilson suffered a loss of power. At the Paris Conference of January, 1919, he met with the leaders of England, France, and Italy and won agreement on his plan for the League of Nations, which was to be included in the Treaty of Versailles. Most of the features of Wilson's plan for the Leage of Nations are today operating in the United Nations. This fact indicates the basic strength of the Wilson plan. But when Wilson returned to America, he discovered tremendous oppostion in the Congress of his own country, particularly in the Senate.

The Versailles Treaty was presented to Congress by Wilson in July, 1919, and was sent to the powerful Senate Committee on Foreign Affairs, which refused to recommend its ratification.

[51]

Determined, Wilson decided to turn to the people. He made long, tiring trips, speaking to huge audiences and explaining the necessity of the League of Nations. His plea was not exclusively for Americans—it was for all people in all countries who hated war. To him, the League of Nations could make World War I the last world war. His trips, however, were cut short when he suffered a mild stroke. He returned to Washington with the knowledge that American membership in the League was doomed. It was a crushing defeat for Woodrow Wilson when the Senate failed to ratify the treaty.

Chapter 6

True to Himself

S oon after the 66th Congress opened, Sam Rayburn took another swing at government control of the railroads. The Committee on Interstate Commerce had reported a bill that included government control of railroad rates and, at the same time, limited the rights of railroad labor unions.

"It seems to me," Rayburn said in a speech before the House, "that it is fundamental that when you rob the railroads of this country of the incentive of competition and service, you have taken away from the railroads the greatest incentive to perform a great public service to the people. It would also be a mistake to . . . penalize every member of the railroad [unions]." In taking this stand, Rayburn demonstrated that he was not on the side of mangement or on the side of labor. What he wanted was justice for the railroads, its workers, and the American public.

A little later in the debates it came out that the powerful labor union leader, Samuel Gompers, had been urging Congressmen to vote for continuing government control of the railroads for an additional two-year period. When the man from Bonham heard of this he thundered at his fellow representatives with a blistering attack on Gompers' influence. "Has it come to pass," Rayburn said, "in this country that the free representatives of a free people can be scared by the threat of Mr. Gompers or anyone else who represents less than five percent of the people of the land?"

Sam Rayburn's stand on the railroad controversy is typical. Throughout his years in Congress, many people found it difficult to say what Sam Rayburn's politics were. He was not a liberal, for he often was against liberal legislation. At the same time he was not a conservative, for at times he was the main spokesman for liberal causes. To those who would try to give him a designation as a "liberal Democrat" or a "conservative Democrat," the reply he gave was classic: "I am a Democrat without prefix or suffix or apologies or handles."

The role of a minority party Congressman was not an easy one for Sam Rayburn, who had come to Congress when the Democrats were riding a wave of popularity across the nation. Men like John Garner helped Rayburn in his days of apprenticeship, and Garner was a powerful force in Congress. Another man who took an interest in Rayburn was the Speaker of the House himself, Champ Clark of Missouri. Neither Garner nor Clark pulled their punches with the new Congressman. Clark told Rayburn flatly that he was a good man, but that he didn't know enough history to be a good lawmaker. He gave Rayburn a list of books he should read, including biographies of several Presidents. Sam Rayburn took all the good advice well.

By 1920, the man from the Fourth District was a mature and able representative with the respect of his fellow Congressmen, both Democratic and Republican. But a Congress is run by the party in power, and Sam Rayburn was forced into a minor role as a member of the minor party. It was natural for him to hope the national election of that year would keep a Democrat in the White House. Equally important was for the Congress to be regained by the Democrats.

In the Fourth District of Texas, Rayburn ran for reelection to his fifth term in the House. His opponent, Ed Westbrook, was swamped in defeat in the primary election. Immediately, Rayburn's interest turned to the national election of 1920.

The Democrats nominated James Cox for President and a young New York politician, Franklin Roosevelt, for vice president. The Republicans chose Warren G. Harding for President and Calvin Coolidge for the second spot on the ticket. In setting up the speaking assignments for the campaign, the chairman of the national Democratic Executive Committee selected Sam Rayburn of Texas to tour the Midwest. He made several of his best speeches in Ohio, the home state of both Presidential candidates. But on his tour through the great heartland of the country, Rayburn sensed what the voters might do in the election. The results at the polls were overwhelming. The Republicans retained control of the Senate and the House. Along with it, they won the Presidency, too, as 16,000,000 citizens voted for Harding while only 9,000,000 voted for Cox. After eight years of Democratic administration under Wilson, the government was Republican.

Under Harding, the Republican 67th Congress seemed to set a goal of undoing the work of the previous Democratic Congresses. One of the first issues to be debated was the tariff. The Republicans favored increasing the tariff, while the Democrats wanted their own Underwood Tariff Act to remain in effect. The debates in the House were as heated as the steaming Washington weather in July 1921, as Rayburn gained the Speaker's recognition and addressed the House.

"The two great Parties," Rayburn said, "are again brought into conflict on the tariff question. [This] has been for many years a question of vital difference between the Democratic and the Republican Parties. This measure brought in at this time makes the issue keener than it has ever been before. The intentions of the two Parties in placing a tariff on imports differ as widely as two views could. The Democratic Party's historic position is and has been that the only reason for the levy and collection of a tariff tax at all is to raise revenue to help pay the expenses of Government, and if any benefit should come to any individual or any industry that benefit is only incidental. The Republican Party's theory is and has been that the reason for the levy of the duty is not to raise revenue but to protect American manufacturers and industries against competition from the outside, and that what revenue is raised is only an incident and not the reason for the tax." Rayburn paused after his simple description of the tariff, with which few could argue. Then, he continued, blasting away now at those who opposed him, "A Democratic tariff would help support the Government and encourage trade and commerce. A Republican tariff would raise little, if any, money for the Government and would [hurt] trade and commerce."

Without doubt, Sam Rayburn made a strong effort for the Democratic tariff. But a new Republican tariff act was certain to pass and be signed into law by President Harding.

During the following months, the man from Fannin County became one of the Democratic party's most eloquent speakers in the Congress. The function of the party out of power is to criticize the action of the party that is in power. To keep some balance in the government, this criticism is even a duty for the minority party. Rayburn performed this well.

Time after time Rayburn stung the opposition with his

[56]

reminder that a peace had not yet been made with Germany and that United States troops remained overseas for no good reason at all. And as Harding's administration continued, there was considerable cause for alarm.

Warren Harding was a handsome man who *looked* like a President. Unfortunately, there was little else to qualify him for the job. As a newspaper editor, state senator, lieutenant governor, and U. S. Senator, Harding had served in a dull and unspectacular manner. Aside from his ability to gather votes, his record was both uninspired and unimpressive. After he became President of the United States, his administration continued to be dull, but at last it became notorious for its general corruption. While Harding was personally honest enough, his judgment of his associates' character was very poor.

Eventually, Director of the Veterans' Bureau Charles R. Forbes was found guilty of misconduct and dishonesty in squandering or stealing $250,000,000 of the Bureau's funds. Attorney General Harry M. Daugherty was charged with criminal neglect of duty and was asked to resign from the Cabinet. A friend of Daugherty's, the alien property custodian, was sentenced to 18 months in prison and fined $5,000 for conspiring to defraud the federal government. By 1922, concern was growing throughout Washington.

Also in 1922, Sam Rayburn was concerned about the wisdom of his remaining in the House of Representatives. As the year began, the news came from Bonham that he would once more be opposed in the Democratic primary by Ed Westbrook, the man he had beaten soundly in 1920. It seemed to Sam Rayburn that after 10 years of representing the people of the Fourth District, it would not be necessary for him to have an opponent on *every* election year.

As Rayburn considered the situation, an obvious answer

presented itself—he could run for the Senate instead of the House. United States Senators are elected for a term of six years. Thus, if Rayburn were elected Senator from Texas he would not have to campaign for reelection as often. Still another reason running for the Senate appealed to Rayburn was the expense involved. In each of his four previous campaigns for the House, Rayburn had spent between $1,500 and $2,000. While the expense of running for the Senate would be much more because the campaign would cover the entire state, it would come less often. As February came, the idea seemed a good one to Rayburn. The men who were considering running for the Senate in Texas were not to be feared at the polls, for Rayburn's reputation had spread far and he already had such friends in the most distant areas of Texas as Jack Garner.

Even Rayburn's friends urged him to run for the Senate, especially as Ed Westbrook's campaign in the Fourth District was looking stronger and stronger. Since Rayburn had created an enemy in the railroad unions with his attack on Gompers' efforts to influence Congressmen, the unions were backing Westbrook. But this one fact made the race in the Fourth District a challenge, and Rayburn perhaps wondered a little if he would be avoiding a fight if he did not meet the challenge. Still, he was being urged to announce his candidacy for the Senate. And now the urging seemed more like an effort to get him out of the House than into the Senate. Before February was over, Rayburn's mind was made up. He would return for what looked like the battle of his life at the polls.

It was a strange campaign. Westbrook used the old political technique of mudslinging. For his part, Sam Rayburn took a new position before the voters of the Fourth. He told them Westbrook could say whatever he pleased, but he—Rayburn—would never stoop to hurting an opponent's feelings or smearing his reputation in order to win any public office. In a sweeping show of political courage, the man from Fannin County told his neighbors he thought the time had come for them to vote according to their conscience. He admitted that his stand against the railroad unions had made enemeies. But for this, he made no apology. Going even further, Rayburn told the voters he would *not* make promises not to offend *any* group, for he felt a man should first of all be true to himself.

When election day came, only one thing was certain: if Rayburn won, the margin would be slim. Rayburn stayed up late that night waiting for the election returns to come, first by "boxes" in the several counties of the Fourth, then finally the county totals themselves.

One by one, the boxes came in and the results were disappointing to the man from Bonham. Some boxes, of course, he expected to lose to Westbrook. But others he felt good about winning. Several of the boxes he thought were safely his fell into the Westbrook column. As he watched late into the night he turned sadly to a friend and said, "I have lost this race."

But the night went on and boxes that should have gone to Westbrook went instead to Rayburn. In others, his lead was a little greater than any had dared to hope. Finally, Rayburn pulled slightly ahead in Fannin County by less than 1,000 votes. When the other county totals were in he had managed to win in each, but the vote was tight and frightening to the last box. In all, his lead over Westbrook was 1,254 votes.

With the victory his, Rayburn at last and happily went to bed. It had been a long day.

Chapter 7

A Prophecy Fulfilled

President Harding, returning from Alaska in July of 1923, became ill in San Francisco and died suddenly. Vice President Calvin Coolidge was called from his home to be sworn into the highest office in the nation. Coolidge, the third president to enter the White House while Sam Rayburn was in the House of Representatives, came into office as the scandals of the Harding administration were growing. Coolidge insisted that his administration should push the investigations of corruption.

President Coolidge quickly won respect that Harding had never been able to achieve. As Coolidge filled out the remainder of Harding's term, the United States enjoyed the "return to normalcy" that people had hoped for in their vote of 1920. Government spending was still fairly high, but business prosperity more than made up for it. Taxes were reduced, and there was even enough left over to reduce the national debt.

The only trouble spot in the economy was the plight of the farmer. Being from the rural area of Texas' Fourth District,

Sam Rayburn had a vital interest in this problem. Two things kept him from hoping to get Congress to make any improvement in the condition of the country's farmers. First, business in general was good; and second, Rayburn was still a member of the minority party in Congress.

Within ten months after President Coolidge took office, thoughts of the 1924 national elections were taking the spotlight throughout the country. For the Republicans, the choice was easy. President Coolidge was popular with the people because the nation was enjoying one of its greatest periods of prosperity. In their national convention in June of 1924, Coolidge was nominated without any opposition.

The convention of the out-of-office Democrats during the same month was another matter. Through 103 ballots, the convention was deadlocked between Governor Alfred E. Smith of New York and William G. McAdoo of California, President Wilson's Secretary of the Treasury. The convention finally realized neither man could win the nomination. John W. Davis of New York, one of Wilson's advisers, won the nomination.

A new political party called the Farmer-Labor party nominated Senator Robert M. LaFollette of Wisconsin. But he drew only 4,822,900 votes compared to Davis's 8,386,500, and both were swamped as President Coolidge received almost 16,000,000 votes. And, in Congress, the Republicans maintained control of both the House and the Senate.

So the situation remained the same for the Democrats. Sam Rayburn had not been surprised to hear that he was being opposed once more in the Democratic primary of the Fourth District. This time, however, there was not the problem of an active and dangerous opponent such as Westbrook. Rayburn put in a brief appearance, made a few speeches, and won his 7th term by over 9,000 votes.

Throughout President Coolidge's administration, Sam Rayburn struggled to get something done to help agriculture, the one weak spot in the nation's economy. After the election the situation became worse. For many years before, European countries had been purchasing much of their food from the United States. As these purchases fell off, farmers were unable to sell their products at a reasonable profit. So, while other industries made money, the farmers were struggling to survive. Tirelessly, Sam Rayburn worked to get legislation passed that would help not only the farmers of his own Fourth District, but farmers throughout the nation as well.

Congress passed several bills that might have worked. Two bills were vetoed by President Coolidge on the grounds that the government should not be involved in business. Each of the bills included a guarantee to farmers that they would receive better prices for their products.

During the debates in the House of Representatives, Rayburn made one of his greatest pleas for consideration of agriculture's important role. "The farmers have been the pioneers in all the advancement of our country," the man from Fannin said. "It was the farmer who went forth to clear away the forests and turn the sod of the prairie to make it a home for man that products may be brought forth to feed and clothe the world. He went into the . . . forest before the railroads . . . or the factories or other businesses went there, and there never would have been railroads and factories or towns if the pioneer farmer had not blazed the way. . . . Every other industry in the land should want agriculture to be prosperous. If the farmers are not prosperous the revenue of the railroads shrinks and labor upon the railroads is idle. If agriculture is not prosperous the smoke will cease to lift from the factories and their business shall perish from the earth, and thousands upon thousands of men and women will be left unable to buy the output of the factories. So, with the merchants and the banks. We are all interdependent upon each other, and if the greatest and most basic of all industries is not prosperous, then every other industry fails to prosper."

Rayburn was a careful student of economics. And when it came to the subject of agriculture, no one spoke with more authority. His remarks on the role of agriculture are historic, for in them was a prediction that a few years later proved true. ". . . the smoke will cease to lift from the factories. . . ."

When President Coolidge vetoed the McNary-Haugen Farm Bill in 1927, there was not enough support for the Congress to override his decision. The farm problem remained and grew worse. As a member of the minority party, Rayburn spoke out often in the House of Representatives; but his voice did not carry the authority it needed to get things done. As Rayburn himself later said, "I didn't amount to much then."

But if Rayburn did not carry authority as an influence in government in 1927, such was not the case with all his affairs. In 1926, he received the surprising news that there would be no candidate opposing him for his seat in the House. So for this first time in eight campaigns, the man from Bonham was unopposed. And this newfound streak of good fortune continued into 1927 with a new and serious romantic interest for Sam Rayburn. The girl was from Valley View, Texas, a small town in the same area as Sam's.

Her name was Metze Jones. Her brother, Marvin, had been a friend of Sam Rayburn for a long time and—like everyone— probably thought of Rayburn as a confirmed bachelor at the age of 45. But 27-year-old Metze caught the Congressman's heart. They were married on October 15, 1927, and spent their honeymoon in the blue hills of Tennesse. Afterward, they returned to Washington for the winter. Sam wrote letters indicating his great happiness with his bride to several friends.

But before the winter was ended, the Rayburn marriage somehow was broken. After only a few months together, Metze and Sam parted. A divorce was granted to Metze in Bonham, and the entire affair was never discussed further by Sam Rayburn. Many people even developed the idea that Rayburn had never been married at all.

One thing, however, is certain. Sam Rayburn entered his marriage full of hope for its success and love for his wife. They were happy for a short time, and the failure of the marriage was a wound from which Rayburn never recovered. Hurt by it, he refused to discuss it, especially with newspapermen who could have used it in a way that would have embarrassed both himself and his former wife. It was a personal affair, and Rayburn was successful in keeping it that way. He turned his attention once more to the business of government.

The year 1928 renewed the everlasting American fascination with national politics. Even in the years of prosperity under Coolidge, people were eager to see an old-fashioned political fight for control of the government. In the national conventions, the Republicans selected Coolidge's Secretary of Commerce, Herbert Hoover, while the Democrats named Alfred E. Smith for President. This time the Democrats were more hopeful, for Smith was selected without any serious opposition at the convention. As the governor of New York, he had proven his ability as an administrator and vote-getter. Rayburn expressed the hope of his party when he said, "My hope and trust is that in the coming election the people will rise up in their might, in their power and elect a President and a Congress that will do its duty and do justice to agriculture, the greatest of all our great industries."

But before the man from Fannin County could focus his full attention on the national election of the fall, there was the business of running for Congress in the Fourth District of Texas. This time there was not just one opponent, but three! Rayburn met the opposition squarely and came out with a majority of over 5,000 votes.

In earlier national elections, the leadership of the Democratic party had asked Rayburn to campaign for the national ticket in areas far removed from his native Texas. But early in the 1928 campaign, the Democrats realized some of their strongest states were slipping away and might actually fall into the Hoover column. Texas was one of the doubtful states, and Rayburn was asked to campaign in his home state.

Several things worked against the Democratic candidate. First, his stand against prohibition hurt him in the Midwest and in the South. Another mark against him was his association with the New York political machine, Tammany Hall. Third—and perhaps most damaging to him—was his religion. As a Catholic, Smith campaigned effectively in New York. But many Protestant groups actually feared that Smith would allow the Catholic church to control his policies if he were elected President. Unfortunately, opposition to a Catholic President was concentrated in the Democratic Southern states.

In Texas, Sam Rayburn attacked the idea that Smith would be influenced by the leaders of his religious faith. Just as it would be dangerous for the government to try to control religion, it would be just as dangerous for any religious group to seek control of the government. Somehow, the people did not believe this in 1928.

When the returns of the election were in, Hoover had carried all but eight states, including Tennessee, Virginia, North Carolina, Florida, and Sam Rayburn's Texas. In all,

Hoover gathered in over 21,000,000 votes, to Smith's 15,000,000, and became the fourth President Sam Rayburn served under in the House.

President Hoover entered the White House early in 1929 with optimistic assurance that the country was in excellent economic condition. He was an able administrator and brilliant thinker, but even brilliant and capable men are sometimes mistaken. Hoover failed to take into proper consideration several facts that pointed in the other direction. First, agriculture was still a serious problem, its income being far behind that of industry. Second, American industry was producing more than it could sell.

Other matters disturbed men like Sam Rayburn in the opening days of the 71st Congress in April of 1929. There had long been a depression in Rayburn's district, and to him it seemed only a matter of time until it would spread to the rest of the nation. But few listened, for Hoover's Republican party continued its control over both houses of Congress.

The shock that a few men such as Sam Rayburn knew was coming arrived in October of 1929. On the 23rd, the stock market suffered an average drop of 18 points. Within a few days, the nation's business came crashing down. This stock market crash marked the beginning of the worst economic depression in the history of the nation.

Still, Hoover and his advisers clung to the belief that American business was as sound as ever. The President said "the fundamental business of the country . . . production and distribution of commodities, is on a sound and prosperous basis." As he spoke factories were closing, and businesses were failing.

Sam Rayburn had said, "the smoke will cease to lift from the factories and their businesses shall perish from the earth."

Chapter 8

Rise to Power

As the Depression moved in 1930, President Hoover continued to be certain that prosperity was "just around the corner." Bravely, the President asserted the traditional American philosophy that dedicated efforts by individual citizens would solve the problem. He was opposed to the government stepping in to help end the Depression, for he still had complete confidence in business solving its own problems. This attitude was reasonable, for the nation's business had never suffered a depression that it had not conquered by itself. As Sam Rayburn later remarked, the 1929 depression would have fallen on any man who happened to be President at the time, whether Democrat or Republican.

In the House of Representatives, the 71st Congress of the United States was once more debating the age-old question of tariffs. This time, another point was raised in the discussion —the desire of the Republicans to have a flexible tariff in which the tax on certain products could be raised or lowered by the President without the approval of Congress. Rayburn and his fellow Democrats, of course, vigorously opposed this measure. Nevertheless, it passed both houses of Congress and was signed into law by President Hoover. But it failed to keep the Depression from growing worse.

In 1930, the depths the Depression eventually would reach were still unknown, even though the people were restlessly wondering about the truth of President Hoover's assurance that it was only temporary. It is just as well that America did not know what was ahead, for the figures became staggering. By the end of 1931, almost 10,000,000 workers were unemployed. Between the years 1929 and 1932, 85,000 businesses closed their doors; their failures involved losses of $4,500,000,000. In 1929, the national income of the United States was $81,000,000,000; by 1931 it was only $53,000,-000,000; and by 1932 it was down to $41,000,000,000.

So, while the worst was yet to come, people still had mixed feelings about the future. Some—even many—agreed with Hoover that the Depression was still only temporary and that prosperity was "just around the corner." Others, like Sam Rayburn, believed the time had arrived for vigorous action by the government to save the nation from self-destruction. Of course, the Depression had hit Rayburn's District earlier than it did much of the country—for agriculture was the first industry to fail. And agriculture was basic to Rayburn's area of North Texas. If the people of the nation were worried, the people in the Fourth District were desperate.

The economy of North Texas was so depressed by the summer of 1930 that the voters could well have considered ending their Congressman's stay in Washington. As a matter of fact, two men, C. B. Randell and B. L. Shirley, paid their filing fee for the July Democratic primary. They began telling the voters of the Fourth that it was time to put someone in Washington who could get something done to help their stricken area. But the people of the District realized that for 12 years their Congressman had been under the thumb of the opposition party, and that another Democrat such as Randell or Shirley was not likely to do any better than Sam Rayburn. In the election Rayburn was returned to the House of Representatives for his tenth consecutive term.

Around the nation, the Republicans lost seats in the House to Democrats, an indication of the growing distrust of the Hoover administration. But the Republicans still maintained control by an extremely slim margin. It appeared that Sam Rayburn would serve another two years under Republican rule. But several Republican members died after the election and before the 72nd Congress met, and the Democratic party discovered that it actually had a majority of four members in the House! After 12 years of working as the minority, the Democratic party moved to reorganize the House of Representatives and elect their own Democratic speaker.

The powerful leader of the Democratic party, John Nance Garner of Uvalde, Texas, took up the Speaker's gavel. At the same time, leadership on the floor of the House was passed to such men as John McCormack of Massachusetts, Fred Vinson of Kentucky, and Sam Rayburn of Texas. As Garner called the House to order, it was doubtless one of the most joyous days in Sam Rayburn's life.

Under Garner, the 72nd Congress was primarily concerned with legislation that would help relieve the economic plight of the country. To its surprise, the Democratic Congress found in President Hoover a sympathetic man. Slowly, Hoover began to realize that the nation was not going to recover from the Depression without help from the government.

[69]

While he was opposed to federal intereference with business, Hoover did not suffer from a closed mind on the subject of federal aid to his country. Conservative Herbert Hoover was the first President in history to attempt federal assistance in pulling the nation out of a depression. At the same time, President Hoover continued to stress the importance of each individual American doing his part to meet the great problem.

But these first efforts by the Congress and by the President were—like most first efforts—not quite enough. Both were learning an entirely new concept of the rule of the federal government in the affairs of the United States. And, of course, learning new concepts takes time. The important thing is that the Congress and the President realized something had to be done—and done quickly. Also, it was necessary for the new programs to be within the limits of the Constitution.

Among the first of Hoover's efforts to improve conditions was his National Credit Association, which helped to protect banks from collapse. Another effort was the change in the policy of the Federal Reserve Board, so that Federal Reserve Banks could lend money to industry at low interest rates for the construction of plant improvements or expansion.

Then, in January of 1932, Hoover sought the approval of still another federal device to help the nation: The Reconstruction Finance Corporation. Known as the RFC, this organization was created to lend money to banks, insurance companies, building and loan associations, railroads, farm credit associations, and industry. As the bill creating the RFC was debated in Congress, it was proposed to give the Corporation a fund of $2,000,000,000 for lending. Before the RFC bill was passed, Sam Rayburn suggested two amendments.

First, Rayburn felt the total amount of money a single borrower could get from the RFC should be limited to $100,-

000,000. This, Rayburn pointed out, would be sufficient to take care of the needs of even the largest corporations. His second amendment was to prevent any agent of a borrower from getting any of the RFC funds. Rayburn wanted to avoid dishonesty by former members of Congress, who might use their influence to obtain a large loan. The former member could then set an extremely high fee for his services.

By the summer of 1932, President Hoover yielded to pressure for giving federal aid for the millions of Americans who were unemployed and without any means to support themselves. President Hoover also approved a program for the use of more than $2,000,000,000 to be given to the individual states of the Union for the construction of public buildings and emergency relief for the unemployed. In 1932, President Hoover was moving in the direction of vigorous government action to overcome the Depression. But two years of hardship under his administration had weakened his popularity.

When serious talk about the Democratic nominee for the Presidential election first began in the capital, Sam Rayburn made it plain that his choice was John Nance Garner, the powerful Speaker of the House of Representatives. But early in the year an organization for Franklin D. Roosevelt was already growing strong. So thorough was Roosevelt's campaign to win the Democratic nomination for President, that many good Democrats resented it. They did not want a "rigged" convention in the summer. "Stop Roosevelt" organizations sprang up throughout the party, and one of the biggest names in the movement was Jack Garner's.

Franklin Roosevelt had campaigned widely and captured the imagination and even the affections of many thousands of the people. After his unsuccessful bid for the vice-presidency on the Cox ticket in 1920, Roosevelt had been stricken with polio. Most people thought his political life was ended. But with the encouragement of his wife and close friends, he returned. When he did, he was stronger politically than he had ever been! He ran for and won the governorship of New York.

In John Garner, Roosevelt found an active and brilliant opponent in his bid for the Democratic nomination. As the Speaker of the House, Garner held the highest office in the legislative branch of the government, equaled only in prestige by the Chief Justice of the Supreme Court and the President himself. For his campaign manager in the weeks before the convention, Jack Garner selected his protégé, Sam Rayburn.

Garner's selection was wise, for before the national convention started in Chicago it became apparent that a deadlock between Garner and Roosevelt was possible—even likely. Garner-for-President clubs were forming throughout America, with enthusiasm running especially high in Garner's own state, Texas. At first, Garner's Texas supporters wanted to put on a big show for their "favorite son" at the national convention —complete with cowboy boots and hats. But Sam Rayburn said no. The Presidency was the most dignified office in the land, and he believed his fellow Texans should so treat it.

A few weeks before the convention, it occurred to the Roosevelt forces that a possible way to avoid an open fight on the floor of the convention would be to offer Jack Garner the vice-presidential nomination if he would, in turn, support Roosevelt for the Presidency. There was no question that Roosevelt controlled more convention votes than Garner. But he needed a few more to win the nomination. James A. Farley was selected by the Roosevelt organization to approach Sam Rayburn on this way to avoid a deadlock at the convention.

But before Farley could get in touch with the man from Fannin County, Cactus Jack Garner heard of the plan. When he did, Garner reminded everyone in the clearest of Texas-type language that he was *not* a candidate for the vice-presidency. Still, Farley continued his efforts to meet with Rayburn. Finally, he agreed to come to Farley's Washington apartment for a meeting.

In his book, *Behind the Ballots, the Personal History of a Politician,* Farley describes the meeting.

". . . I used all the salesmanship at my command to convince them of the necessity for a combination of Roosevelt-Garner forces. I pointed out that the New York Governor would have a substantial majority over all his opponents combined on the first ballot and that by all the rules of the game he was entitled to the nomination without delay. A parallel situation had taken place at Houston in 1928 when Al Smith had a majority, and his opponents had graciously given way and permitted his nomination without further contest. I recalled that Governor Roosevelt and Speaker Garner were personal friends and had always thought highly of one another. I pointed out the obvious fact that the first delegation to see the light of reason would naturally be in a strategic position if it switched over to our side and assured the Governor's nomination. The Texas delegation with its 46 votes was big enough to do the job even without California. And then came the big moment—I promised to do everything in my power to secure the vice-presidential nomination for Speaker Garner if Texas made the switch."

Silently, Sam Rayburn watched Farley as he spoke, listening to and weighing each word carefully. And the man from Bonham did not change the expression of his face as Farley made the offer of the vice-presidency for Jack Garner. Rayburn's answer was brief, but it was packed with meaning for the Roosevelt forces. Farley reported Rayburn's statement:

[73]

"We have come to Chicago to nominate Speaker Jack Garner for the Presidency if we can. We are not against any other candidate and we are not for any other candidate. Governor Roosevelt is the leading candidate and naturally he must be headed off if we are to win. But we don't intend to make it another Madison Square Garden."

In these words, Jim Farley had his answer. Rayburn knew that Garner would come into the convention with about 180 delegates backing him. Rayburn fully intended to make a fight for the Presidential nomination. At the same time, he recognized that Garner and Roosevelt were friendly and he made it plain that the Garner forces were not *against* Roosevelt—they simply were *for* Garner. Rayburn himself liked Franklin Roosevelt. He remembered fondly having talked with him on the telephone when Roosevelt was Wilson's undersecretary of the Navy. Rayburn's impression at the time was that Roosevelt was one of the most pleasant men in Washington to deal with. So —with the convention approaching in a matter of days—Sam Rayburn was careful not to burn his bridges behind him and thus leave a possible vice-presidential nomination for Jack Garner on the other side. This position he made plain with his statement that "we don't intend to make it another Madison Square Garden"—the scene of the Democratic convention of 1924 where the long, tiresome, and futile 103-ballot battle between Smith and McAdoo had taken place.

The meeting between Farley and Rayburn was secret, for knowledge in the convention of friendly conversations between opponents could do tremendous damage to both Roosevelt and Garner. When the convention was called to order in Chicago, Sam Rayburn was the only man present who had a direct line of communication to Jack Garner. It was understood between them that Garner would make a fight for the Presidential nomination but would not throw the convention into a long deadlock. Garner and Rayburn agreed that it would not be right to put individual ambition over the welfare of the Democratic party and the future of the United States.

Sam Rayburn and Jim Farley met a second time at Chicago when the convention was getting under way. But this meeting was not quite so secret as the first. Farley recalls that he went to the Garner headquarters and met with Rayburn briefly. This time, Farley made his offer of the vice-presidency even more firmly than he had earlier.

Stripping away all the frills, Rayburn then asked Roosevelt's representative exactly what Roosevelt wanted them to do. Farley answered with honesty:

"Have the Texas delegation record its vote for Garner on the first ballot, and then before the result is announced switch to Roosevelt. I feel certain that some state will make the break after it becomes apparent that the Governor has a big majority, and Texas might as well be first."

It was an attractive offer and a reasonable request, for Roosevelt had a definite majority and Garner had only an outside chance of winning. Even so, the opposition to Roosevelt was a little frightening; for there was a hard core of Garner supporters at the convention. Farley admitted the Roosevelt delegates might begin to break away to some other candidate if Roosevelt were not nominated by the fifth ballot on the convention. This is a general sort of rule in political conventions. If a candidate does not win early—or show good signs of winning—his followers become discouraged and are likely to hop on a "bandwagon" for another candidate. Rayburn's and Garner's position at the Democratic convention of 1932 was based on this idea. If they could hold their delegates long enough— through perhaps three ballots—a Garner bandwagon could break Roosevelt's majority and give the Presidential nomination to the Speaker.

Again, Rayburn listened carefully to Farley's statement. Then, the man from Bonham explained his own position. The delegates who wanted Garner were eager to fight for his nomination. It would not be fair to them for Texas to desert the cause in the middle of the first ballot. So, there was no choice but to keep Garner's name before the convention for the first few ballots, even if the vice-presidency offer were accepted. And, Rayburn hastened to add, Garner was *not* saying he was interested in the vice-presidency at all, at that particular time. In fact, no mention of it had been made to Speaker Garner, for he had already made it clear that he preferred the power of his position as Speaker of the House of Representatives.

After three ballots on the first night of voting, Roosevelt was no nearer the necessary number of votes required for nomination. There was a clear majority in favor of the New York governor, but that was not enough. Worried that some of the delegates might break away on the next morning's ballot, the Roosevelt group under Farley again began to look for Sam Rayburn to help them. They met that night and no further mention was made of the vice-presidency for Jack Garner, only that Roosevelt needed the Texas vote to break the convention's deadlock. Rayburn had already stated that he did not want another deadlocked convention; and further, he and Garner had agreed that this would be bad for the Democrats in the fall election. Once more, Rayburn listened to the Roosevelt request for help from the Texas delegation. Then, without committing himself or Jack Garner, he told them he would see what he could do.

At the same time, Jack Garner decided to withdraw his name from the race for the Presidential nomination. With no thought of the vice presidency, Garner pointed out that the convention favored Roosevelt and that he felt the New York governor should receive the nomination on the next ballot. In his telephone conversation with Rayburn, Jack Garner officially released the Texas and California delegations from voting for him on the next ballot.

Rayburn called for a caucus, a meeting of the members of the Texas delegation to the convention. It turned out to be quite a fight for the man from Bonham because many delegates could not believe Garner was withdrawing from the race. As Rayburn later recalled, the meeting turned into quite an argument, with some of the women delegates actually crying over Garner's decision. Others felt the Texas delegation should continue to vote for Garner anyway.

As the argument among the Texas delegation went on and on, Sam Rayburn finally had had enough. He forced a vote on the issue and the delegation decided—54 to 51—to vote for Roosevelt on the next ballot. This result in itself was a victory for Rayburn, for many of the delegates preferred other men than Roosevelt if they could not have their "favorite son."

With the first victory won in his own Texas delegation, the man from Fannin County moved quickly. He informed the leader of the California delegation that Garner had dropped out of the race and that Texas was voting for Roosevelt. It was only a short time until California was released from Garner to Roosevelt, and his nomination was certain.

As it turned out, Garner's decision came in the nick of time. One of the strongest Roosevelt states was Mississippi, and it was about to break away from the Roosevelt camp when the news came that Texas and California had both switched their votes. The news that these two states with their large number of votes were now going to Roosevelt kept Mississipppi in line.

The other Roosevelt states held firm too, and the convention named him as its candidate for President on the next ballot.

Still, there was no talk of Jack Garner for vice president—at least none was directed to the Speaker himself. When it was made clear to Rayburn that Garner was Roosevelt's own choice, the man from Bonham called his fellow-Texan. The theory behind the preference for Garner was that he would make the perfect counterbalance for Roosevelt on the national Democratic ticket. Garner's reputation was more conservative than Roosevelt's, and Garner had more appeal to the millions of rural voters. In the Southern states, Garner's name would have much influence and help hold them fast for the Democratic party. In 1928, several of the key Southern states had voted for Hoover, and the Democrats were eager to recover these losses in the 1932 election. Carefully, Rayburn explained these reasons for Garner's taking the vice presidential nomination.

In the end, Jack Garner left the decision pretty much in Sam Rayburn's hands. The older man trusted his younger friend's knowledge of the situation. And even though Garner preferred the important post of Speaker of the House of Representatives, he agreed to run for the vice presidency if Rayburn were convinced it would actually help elect a Democrat President. Garner's name was placed in nomination before the convention, and with the backing of Roosevelt delegates, Garner won the nomination on the first ballot.

As the Democratic national convention of 1932 closed, not a delegate present was unaware of the tremendous influence Rayburn had wielded throughout the session. His action to a great extent was responsible for the number of ballots taken, the timing of Roosevelt's victory, and the selection of the party's nominee for vice president of the United States.

Sam Rayburn had arrived in 1932.

Chapter 9

Starting on the Long Way Back

The good people of the Fourth Congressional District of Texas voted Sam Rayburn into the Congress of the United States 25 consecutive times. They were, Rayburn said, 98½ percent good and honest folks who would do the right thing when they were presented with the facts. As it turned out, the people of the Fourth decided on most occasions to call their Representative back to the District for a heated campaign against one or more opponents. In this way, they got the facts on a regular basis. For as Rayburn's reputation in Washington grew, his reputation in the Fourth was continually questioned by those who would take his job away from him. The year 1932 was not an exception.

In his race for an 11th term in the House, the man from Fannin County was opposed by Jess Morris, a newspaperman from Greenville. His second opponent was the former Congressman from the area, Choice B. Randell of Sherman. Both Greenville and Sherman are larger than Rayburn's hometown,

Bonham, and there was a strong feeling Morris and Randell could at least split the vote and force a runoff election.

As the campaign started, both opponents attacked Rayburn's personal and professional activities, particularly Jess Morris, who resorted to the old mudslinging tactics of Texas political races. He drew large crowds for his speeches, and the people of the Fourth laughed heartily as he described the large Rayburn family home near Bonham as a "mansion." With the District still in the depths of the Depression, this seemed to be a good point. Morris claimed that Rayburn associated with the rich folks in Washington, as well as at home. He also pointed out that Rayburn's 20 years in Congress was a long time, too long in fact. The man from Bonham had been paid $200,000 in salary by the taxpayers, Morris said, again giving emphasis to Rayburn's personal prosperity in contrast to the lot of the people in the District who were suffering from the Depression. And, in a final burst of mudslinging at its worst, Morris pointed out that he was even a *larger* man than Sam Rayburn.

The crowds laughed as Morris repeatedly slammed into Rayburn's reputation and appearance. With such a reaction, Morris probably thought he might win a landslide victory. But he didn't know that many in his audience were laughing *at* him instead of *with* him. For his part, Rayburn answered the charges made against him. Jokingly, he observed that using a tape measure or scales to evaluate a man's ability in Congress was a pretty poor idea. The people of the Fourth agreed, for Rayburn got almost 18,000 votes to Morris's 10,000. The third candidate, Randell, had just under 7,000.

To Sam Rayburn, this was quite a relief; for July was the beginning of the national campaign for Roosevelt and Garner. In the middle of the month, Jim Farley sent Rayburn a wire at his home, asking him for his advice and help in the campaign.

Before he hit the campaign trail across the nation in support of Roosevelt and Garner, Sam Rayburn went to Warm Springs, Georgia, for his first personal meeting with the Democratic candidate. When the visit was finished, the man from Bonham was convinced the Democratic party might once more win the White House. The Republican party renominated President Hoover on the first ballot. But the Democrats sensed their moment had arrived. Speeches by Franklin Roosevelt, Jack Garner, Rayburn, and other Democrats were reaching the hearts of the people in the time of their greatest need.

As the Republicans watched, they doubtless wondered how the Democrats were able to achieve such unity. This has been, as a matter of fact, one of the political "puzzles" of modern politics in America. The basic differences between the two great parties lies in the Republican's role as the conservative party, favoring few federal controls, while the Democratic party has slowly developed as the liberal party, favoring federal controls and action wherever and whenever it seems necessary for the good of the country. But the differences go even further and become rather difficult to understand.

One of the best examples of the complexity of the Democratic party appears in its 1932 candidates, Franklin Roosevelt and John Garner. Roosevelt was from Hyde Park, New York, and was related to a former Republican president, Theodore Roosevelt. A member of a family of wealthy landowners and merchants, F.D.R. might be, in United States terms, called "aristocratic." Garner, on the other hand, was from the Texas' blackland prairies with a background much like Rayburn's. Neither man changed. Roosevelt always remained the dignified, Harvard-educated aristocrat from Hyde Park. Garner, while Speaker and later as Vice President, remained a product of the tough country of his home state. And Sam Rayburn, a major campaigner throughout the nation, was much the same type as Garner. Both had been born in a log cabin. Yet all three were Democrats and in fundamental agreement on what the government should do to help the nation.

With the passing years, the Democrats have enjoyed amazing success in attracting totally different types of voters. In the North, the major industrial centers vote Democratic, believing the Democratic party favors labor. In the South, farmers vote Democratic because they believe the party favors agriculture. Large groups of Negroes vote for the Democrats, feeling the party will help give them the equality guaranteed by the Constitution. At the same time, the Deep South has voted for the Democrats in the belief that they would save their historic position of separating the races. This party, then—a great, confused mass of individuals that somehow accepted one another as having the same goals of a better America— came together at last in 1932 and elected Franklin Roosevelt.

The popular vote was 22,821,513 for FDR and 15,761,-787 for President Hoover. Hoover carried only six states with 59 electoral votes to Roosevelt's 472. To the Democrats, it was a marvelous victory; for even their last President, Woodrow Wilson, had never won a majority of the popular votes. The Democrats were in power, not only in the White House but in the Senate and House of Representatives as well.

Sam Rayburn looked forward eagerly to the 73rd Congress of the United States. While he did not pay much attention, there were even rumors in Washington that Rayburn would be elected majority leader of the House, or possibly even Speaker, now that Jack Garner was moving on to the vice presidency. However it might turn out, Rayburn at last was a senior member of the House and was accepted as one of its most powerful and influential voices.

[82]

As a member since 1913, Sam Rayburn's pattern of daily activities was well established, and he did not consider making any changes now that he was one of Congress' most prominent men. Usually, the representative of the Fourth District was in his office early. He spent his mornings answering mail, filling requests from the people in the Fourth, and attending committee meetings, mostly as Chairman of the Committee on Interstate and Foreign Commerce. The people who wrote to him always received a prompt and personal reply. As a matter of policy, Rayburn instructed his office staff to always give him first those letters that were written by hand, rather than typed. These handwritten notes, often scrawled on ruled tablet paper, received Rayburn's close attention. He knew these people were his friends at home and that they would not write to him if it were not something important. By 1932, it was not uncommon for Rayburn to receive a good deal of his day's mail from areas outside the Fourth District and even from many other states than Texas. Over the years he had built a reputation for being interested in people, no matter where they were from; and if they had a problem, he was happy to help find a solution.

The 73rd Congress opened its first session early in March, 1933, with a program from the new President ready for its consideration. Rayburn reminded his fellow Congressmen that the program the people of the United States were looking for and waiting for was the program of Franklin Roosevelt. The Congress did not keep them waiting long, for in the weeks that followed a huge volume of legislation from President Roosevelt was passed by Congress and signed into law by him. Many have called the 73rd a "rubber stamp" Congress for this reason. Perhaps it was—or perhaps it was simply in total agreement with the man who was in the White House in 1933. Roosevelt promised a "New Deal," and the Congress cooperated.

The first consideration of Roosevelt's administration was a series of emergency programs to relieve the pressures of the Depression. Held back for a time were some of the sweeping reforms in the federal government that were to become the most famous parts of Roosevelt's administration. Mostly, his action in the early days of 1933 was an extension and quickening of the philosophy that President Hoover had finally accepted—that the government would *have* to do something to help the nation recover from the Depression. Because of his background and his basic beliefs, Hoover had had a more limited program than Roosevelt's. The new President pushed forward with the most vigorous program of federal action the nation has ever seen in its history, never equaled before and never approached since.

THE SAM RAYBURN LIBRARY

Congressman Rayburn and Senator Clarence C. Dill (Dem., Wash.) watched President Roosevelt sign the Emergency Railroad Act, 1933.

[84]

To help national recovery, Congress passed quickly Roosevelt's Emergency Banking Act. The President announced a "bank holiday" in which all the nation's banks were closed between March 5 and 9. The act Congress passed gave the President the power to completely reorganize any national bank that was in serious financial difficulty. The Federal Emergency Relief Administration extended even more aid to the millions of unemployed persons in the country who were unable to find work. And, to help persons who were unable to make mortgage payments on their homes, the Home Owners' Loan Corporation was formed, with $3,000,000,000 for loans.

The three most dramatic efforts of the Roosevelt administration were the Civilian Conservation Corps, known as the CCC; the National Recovery Administration, the NRA, and the Agricultural Adjustment Act, the AAA. All were drastic measures to help the country, and all had severe faults. But, for the urgent days of 1933, they worked.

The first, the CCC, provided work for unemployed young men. They were sent to huge camps in the national parks and forests. They were also used in clearing out some of the remaining wilderness areas still left in the country. The NRA had broader and more sweeping aims to help the nation. It developed codes for each of America's industries to eliminate unfair competitive practices, abolish child labor, and establish minimum wages. At the same time, certain NRA codes also established short working hours so that more people could be employed. Unfortunately, many businesses could not afford to pay two people to do one job. The overall result was that the NRA was generally ineffective in helping end the Depression.

The program for recovery, however, that drew the keenest attention of Sam Rayburn was the Agricultural Adjustment Act, which became law with President Roosevelt's signature in

May of 1933. Briefly, the AAA provided for a lowering in production of such farm products as wheat, cotton, corn, rice, tobacco, and hogs. All were being produced in far greater supply than the country could either use or sell to foreign nations. Thus, prices for these products had fallen so low that the farmers throughout the nation could no longer make a profit.

Under the AAA, the federal government agreed to pay farmers money for reducing the number of acres planted, and for reducing the number of livestock raised. In addition, the government offered to pay farmers who planted grass on the unfarmed land so that the soil would be covered and not produce dust storms. Immediately the AAA was the greatest help agriculture in the United States has ever enjoyed. Payments to the farmers for producing less helped to ease their money problems quickly. Then, with less products available for sale, prices began to climb back to a level that was profitable for the farmers. For example, the price of cotton—a major crop in Sam Rayburn's Fourth District—almost doubled as a result of the AAA. The program was a success in its first year of operation.

Changes in the AAA were made, however, that eventually caused it to be declared unconstitutional by the Supreme Court. But Rayburn continued to believe the AAA was the best farm program the nation ever had; for the AAA did the job it was supposed to do.

The Democrats—and Sam Rayburn—were happier than they had been in many, many years. Even if some mistakes were made, the government of the United States was at last providing the nation with true leadership.

Chapter 10

Heading for Bigger Things

The year 1934 brought the expected challenge to Sam Rayburn's seat in the House, again from Jess Morris. This time, however, the man from Bonham beat Morris by more than 8,-000 votes, giving Rayburn a 12th term in Congress. His fellow representatives expected that he would win, for his reputation in Capitol Hill was now secure. It might even have come as a surprise to many if they had known how regular and how heated were Rayburn's every-other-year fights to keep his job. Many members with as long a period of service as Sam Rayburn were able to stay in Congress year after year, being re-elected by their districts with no opposition at all. The people of the Fourth were different. As Rayburn grew in importance throughout the country, he was called back home time after time to prove to the voters that he should remain in Washington as their representative. It is, perhaps, a compliment to the people of the Fourth, for even with a man such as Sam Rayburn they still wanted to take a look and make up their minds.

These campaigns helped Rayburn, too, for they kept him in constant touch with the needs and desires of the people of his District. During the months when Congress was not in session, he always returned to his home just outside Bonham to spend the happiest days of the year working on the family farm. In addition to a large cotton crop, the Rayburn farm had developed a dairy herd of outstanding Jersey cattle. The people of the Fourth knew they could find Fannin County's most famous citizen easily, and they came to him often to discuss their problems. But the regular campaigns for office brought the entire situation into clear focus.

One of Rayburn's closest friends in Fannin County was the agricultural agent for the county, Valton Young. In his book, *The Speaker's Agent,* he has recalled a little talk Rayburn made at his home outside Bonham to some of his constituents in the Fourth. Rayburn's remarks reflected his deep feeling and understanding of the problems farmers faced at the time. Rayburn said: "As you know, agriculture has some very great needs. These needs must be met in order to help bring back the whole country to better standards of living. The good people will go along with such a program, I believe. You know, in order to get along, a person sometimes has to go along. That does not imply that anybody ever has to become a rubber stamp, because when two minds always agree, one of them is doing all the thinking. But where there is an umpire in the game and a ruling is made, I learned in baseball that it is a poor player who becomes angry, throws his bat at the umpire, and quits the game like a spoiled child."

From these remarks, Rayburn's foes always quoted only one part—"to get along, a person sometimes has to go along." This quoting out of context was unfortunate, for Rayburn made a far larger and more important point than this.

Continuing, Rayburn explained some of the things he hoped to accomplish to help the farmers of the Fourth District and of the entire nation: "The rural homes must have an opportunity to become more attractive and have more conveniences. Drudgery, darkness, and muddy roads are not conducive to anything that is good. They are not profitable in a democracy. Conveniences will eliminate the feeling of drudgery in the necessary rural tasks that must be done each day. We have enough low-cost power now going to waste in our muddy streams, our best engineers say, to light all the rural homes in America. I simply hate to think of the social, the economic, and the moral loss to about one-third of the people of my State who live on roads that will not permit travel so much of the time to market, to school, to church, and to obtain a doctor for the sick. All-weather roads and rural electricity will drive mud and darkness away in more ways than one."

It was a great hope that eventually would be worked into a great plan by Rayburn. But agriculture was not his only concern in those early days of the New Deal. His hopes for improvement touched on such other areas as the oil industry, public utilities, and the Wall Street stock market. To all of these subjects, Rayburn brought an approach that in many ways was puzzling to his fellow Congressmen. It was an unusual mixture of the conservative and the liberal views of government.

Sam Rayburn's home state is basically conservative in that the people have always desired to have the least possible interference from the federal government. Texans intend to handle their own affairs. And, as a Texan from his earliest days, Sam Rayburn grew up in this tradition. It was and still is a basic attitude in Texas, one that goes all the way back to the area's original settling by Americans who drifted down from Tennessee and other states when Texas was a part of Mexico. These people did not accept Mexico's federal government and proved their independent attitude by declaring Texas an independent republic and starting a revolutionary war against the government of Mexico. Later, when Texas entered the United States, it did so as a recognized nation of the world, and admission to the Union was agreed to by a treaty between the two countries. As time went on, Texas continued to think of its true government as being centered in Austin as much as in Washington. This was the historic background that Sam Rayburn inherited.

To it, he added an important ingredient: his understanding of the modern world. While it was always his preference that matters be handled by local, county, or state governments, Rayburn quickly realized it is not possible in all things. For this reason, he frequently voted for legislation that favored federal action in affairs of the nation. But where it was possible for the state government to handle its problems effectively, he was opposed to any interference from Washington. Unfortunately, there were few things in the early days of the New Deal that could be handled by the individual states. Rayburn agreed with President Roosevelt that the government in Washington had to act if the country was ever to pull out of the Depression.

Already, Rayburn had demonstrated this attitude with his voting record on agricultural problems. And he took the same position on most of the other legislation of the New Deal. With reference to Jack Garner and Sam Rayburn, President Roosevelt remarked, "I like the way those two Texans perform."

A good example of Rayburn's performance in support of the President's program was his Federal Securities Act and, a little later, his Securities Exchange Act of 1934. In both these bills, Rayburn was seeking a way to protect the people who invested their money in corporations. The Federal Securities Act required each corporation to make its financial condition public so that investors would not be tricked into buying worthless securities. In the Securities Exchange Act, additional provisions were made to protect investors.

These bills show Rayburn's interest in having federal controls when there is a definite need. The other side is shown by his attitude toward federal control as proposed in the oil industry bill, which he and Vice President Garner opposed vigorously in 1934. In a long battle, Rayburn and Garner managed to keep control of the oil industry in the hands of the state governments. It was their opinion that state governments were able to handle their own oil industry.

As the 74th Congress of the United States met in January of 1935, Sam Rayburn's interest in a favorite subject was still keen: protecting the people from large corporations that might try to take advantage of them. His earlier Securities bills paved the way for one of Sam Rayburn's most important pieces of legislation: the Public Utilities Holding Company Act of 1935, known in Congress as the Wheeler-Rayburn Bill.

Early in the year, President Roosevelt had sent a proposal to Congress for a law to regulate the nation's public utilities. With his earlier experience, it was natural that in the House of Representatives Sam Rayburn would be the author of the bill. On several occasions, Roosevelt called the man from Fannin County to the White House for discussions on this new and controversial bill. For many years, holding companies had been using loopholes in the antitrust laws to gain control over several public utility companies. As part of his investigation, Sam Rayburn discovered that one man in New York City was serving as an officer in more than 200 separate corporations. Through the system of holding companies, billions of dollars of stock were being controlled by just a few men with very small investments of their own money. In another instance,

Rayburn pointed out that a single banking house in New York owned several huge holding companies, and therefore controlled the price of electricity in one-fourth of all the electric power companies of America. To Rayburn, it seemed unfair for a few men to control so much of other people's money.

Even so, Rayburn wanted to make it plain that he was not the enemy of big business. To the president of the New York Stock Exchange, he said, "I am not an enemy of your business. I think the sale of stocks and bonds is as honorable a business as a man can be engaged in. What I want to do is to take the desperadoes out of your field who have been disgracing what otherwise would have been a clean and honest business in the minds of the people."

Rayburn's bill was passed in the House and in the Senate and was signed into law by President Roosevelt in August of 1935. For Rayburn it had been a far-reaching decision. A few years earlier, the man from Bonham had felt the anger of the labor unions and had almost been defeated as they poured thousands of dollars into an effort to get him out of the House of Representatives. Now many businessmen turned their anger on him. The only difference was that labor unions seemed to be a little more forgiving than Wall Street—as big business was known. Rayburn's position was established with the passage of his bill. Many of his former friends in business fell away, never to forgive or forget.

Still, the man from Bonham stuck to his guns. On a nationwide radio broadcast, Sam Rayburn blazed away: "It was a battle against the biggest and boldest, the richest and the most ruthless lobby Congress has ever known." When the holding companies threatened to take the new law to the Supreme Court, Rayburn fired again. This was no longer a quiet young Congressman. This was one of the powerful voices of the

United States. He warned the Supreme Court in straight Fannin County language that if it should try to restrict the power of the Congress there would still be a way! Congress, Rayburn warned darkly, would tax the holding companies "out of existence." Going further, Rayburn stated firmly this was "warning enough to those who rashly think . . . the American people must be gouged, and bullied . . . forever."

Just as it had not worried Rayburn to have labor unions angry at him, he gave no thought to the disadvantages of enduring the new wrath of businessmen. So, as the next session of the 74th Congress began in early 1936, he turned his attention to the realization of one of his fondest dreams. He began working on a plan to help provide electricity for the thousands of farm families in the nation.

In 1935, President Roosevelt had established the Rural Electrification Administration (REA) under the Emergency Relief Appropriation Act. It had been his plan for $100,000,-000 to be used for rural electrification, but only a small part of this amount was made available. Rayburn intended to come up with a bill that would work—that would put electricity into the farm homes of the country. Many thousands of homes were still lighted by kerosene lamps. But there was, of course, severe opposition to Rayburn's plan. Once again, Rayburn's angry critics included some of the nation's largest corporations.

"Socialist!" they screamed at the man from Fannin County in North Texas. But the utility companies had failed to meet the need. Many tried to get the farmers to pay for a large share of the cost of putting in the power lines, and few farmers could afford the expense. Rayburn pointed out that among 30,000 farm homes in the Fourth District, only about 600 were receiving electric service from the area's utility company. This, he said, showed the companies were not doing a very good job.

As part of Rayburn's bill, low-interest loans from the Rural Electrification Administration would allow farmers to set up co-operatives that would supply electric service through their own transmission lines at low cost. At the same time, farmers were urged to use public utility companies wherever their service was available to them, rather than form a co-operative through REA. President Roosevelt agreed it was a good bill that would help thousands of farm families, and he gave it the full support of his administration. It passed both houses of Congress and was signed promptly by the President.

Looking back on the value of his program to bring electric service to the nation's farm homes, Rayburn later recalled that he had been handicapped by not having electricity in the old Rayburn family home at Flag Springs. "And," he said, "during my mature years, I observed [these] drawbacks from the great dairy farms of the East to the scattered cowboy bunkhouses of the lonely Southwest, and from the fertile farmlands of the Middle West to the often dismal tenant houses of what was formerly known as the Old South." In these comments, Sam Rayburn's interest in the entire nation is revealed. His interest in rural electrification sprang from his own experience in the Fourth District, but he applied it to the improvement of the whole country.

"Throughout the length and breadth of our land," Rayburn said, "a new rural community life has sprung up, bespeaking the wonders that electrical service has wrought. . . . I am proud to have had a part in this movement that made life brighter for church, school, and playground." Obviously, Sam Rayburn was proud of the great accomplishment of the REA program. More than any other man, he pulled the switch that illuminated the nation's farms and brought to them the many conveniences that had long been taken for granted in the cities.

[94]

Though Sam Rayburn did not know it at the moment, his work was soon to be rewarded by his party and by the country. For 23 of his 54 years, the man from Fannin County had served in the Congress of the United States. Under Woodrow Wilson he had "learned the ropes" and had begun to form—through his Stock and Bond Bill—a plan that would prevent large corporations from taking unfair advantage of the people. Then, under Republican Presidents Harding, Coolidge, and Hoover, he had learned the uneasy role of being in the minority. These were difficult years in which Rayburn worked hard, made numerous speeches in the House, but was unable to get his ideas listened to by the majority of members. The tide had changed just before the end of Hoover's administration. With Jack Garner elected Speaker, Rayburn's influence rose and finally came into its full force under the administration of Franklin Roosevelt. After two years of the New Deal, Sam Rayburn was the Democratic party's most eloquent spokesman in the legislative branch of the government. And as the 74th Congress closed its second session on June 20 of 1963, there was no doubt that Sam Rayburn was headed for bigger things than just continuing as plain "Mr. Rayburn of Texas."

Chapter 11

Majority Leader

Afer the close of Congress in June, the rest of 1936 turned out to be one of the busiest periods in Sam Rayburn's life. That summer the Democratic national convention and his own candidacy for a 13th term in the House of Representatives kept him busy. Later there was the steady rumor that the man from Fannin might well become one of the leaders of the Democrats in the House, either as majority leader or as the Speaker.

Already Rayburn was the most widely known Congressman. Young men who were interested in politics often wrote him for advice. Rayburn always replied promptly and went straight to the point. He suggested that the prospective politician should take careful stock of himself, determining exactly his strength and his weaknesses. Rayburn explained that a successful candidate should know his constituents well and pointed out that it was important to have friends who would donate their time and money to help with the election. And he made it clear that the candidate for Congress himself would have to spend a substantial amount of his own money in making the race. Rayburn also reminded those who wrote him that it was expensive to maintain two homes, one in Washington and one in his district. In all, it was not an easy life that Sam Rayburn described for the young and ambitious would-be lawmaker. But he always explained the rich awards of serving in the House of Representatives. "I would rather," Rayburn wrote, "link my name indelibly with the living pulsing history of my country and not be forgotten entirely after a while than to have anything else on earth."

In July 1936, he was forced to fight off two men who would have liked to take this membership from him. Rayburn stood firmly on the accomplishments of the New Deal and reminded the voters of the Fourth District that they should vote for him as long as he was right. "When I am wrong," Rayburn said, "then vote against me." The people of the Fourth thought Sam Rayburn was right, for they cast almost 31,000 votes for him. His nearest opponent, Jess Morris, received about 13,000, leaving little doubt as to Rayburn's popularity.

In the national political conventions, the Democrats renominated Franklin Roosevelt and John Garner, and the Republicans nominated Governor Alf Landon of Kansas. Sam Rayburn of Texas was chosen to direct the National Speakers Bureau for the Democrats, a job involving the selection and scheduling of Democratic speakers to the parts of the country where they could help the national candidates most. It was a smoothly run campaign, and the candidates stood on their record during the first years of the New Deal. Meanwhile, the Republicans seemed to suffer from the same sort of indecision that had plagued the Democrats a few years earlier. Just as the nation's prosperity under Harding and Coolidge had confused the Democrats, the recent success of the Roosevelt administration seemed to befuddle the Republicans. At the polls on November 3, the Democratic candidates ran up an overwhelming majority with an electoral vote of 523 to 8.

In the 75th Congress, the Democrats had increased their majority by a substantial number in both the House of Representatives and the Senate. When the time came for the two parties to appoint their leaders, interest mounted concerning selection of majority leader. In the House the true leader of the party with the most members is elected to the office of Speaker. But the majority party always selects a member to lead its activities on the floor. One of the reasons for this is the nature of the Speaker's job, which has definite duties to provide fair treatment for both Democrats and Republicans alike.

In the 75th Congress, William B. Bankhead of Alabama was certain to be named Speaker. But a sharp battle for Democratic leadership on the floor was shaping up between two men —Sam Rayburn of Texas and John O'Connor of New York.

Rayburn, of course, was intensely interested when it became apparent that he was one of the contenders for the floor leadership. His own aims had long since gone beyond merely serving continuously as another Congressman. In fact, his intention now was to someday sit in the huge Speaker's chair itself. Being elected majority leader would be a step toward his greatest ambition. But he was not confident of election.

Jack Garner had done his best a few years earlier as vice president to get Rayburn elected Speaker. Usually Garner was able to win in political battles of this sort, but Senator Joseph F. Guffey controlled the Pennsylvania delegation in the House from his own position in the Senate. And Guffey did not want Rayburn for Speaker. The position went instead to Joe Byrns, the choice of Guffey's large Pennsylvania group in the House. But—Guffey had not heard the last from Garner.

John O'Connor presented serious opposition to Rayburn's candidacy for the leadership in 1937. In addition to an excellent reputation in the Congress, O'Connor had even served as the temporary leader in the last Congress. But the greatest advantage O'Connor seemed to have was his connection with President Roosevelt himself. For O'Connor's brother was a former partner in Franklin Roosevelt's law firm.

As the battle lines were drawn, Cactus Jack Garner moved again to his friend's side. This action doubtless affected the President's decision not to aid O'Connor. Then, in another move, the Garner influence came down in full force on Senator Guffey of Pennsylvania. O'Connor had helped Guffey on several occasions, and he fought hard for the powerful Senator's support. But between the two, Garner was by far the more

The new House majority leader conferred with Speaker Bankhead.

powerful man, and Guffey swung the Pennsylvania representatives into Rayburn's camp. As the Democratic members of Congress prepared to meet in their caucus to name the majority leader, Sam Rayburn seemed to be pulling away in the lead.

The first state to jump on Rayburn's bandwagon was Louisiana, Texas' neighbor to the east. Others followed quickly as the large Pennsylvania and Texas delegations voted for the man from Bonham. The final vote was 184 to 127.

During the following months in the 75th Congress, Rayburn worked harder than perhaps he ever had before. In addition to his regular duties, it was now Rayburn's job to be the Democrats' principal spokesman on the floor of the House. Beside making many more speeches than usual, he was also responsible for the Democrats' strategy in getting their bills passed by the House. So tireless were his efforts and so thorough was his work in handling his party's goals in Congress, that "Mr. Rayburn" became known by another name that was destined to be his alone for the rest of his life. He became, in addition to Mr. Rayburn, "Mr. Democrat" in the House. The name caught on throughout the United States.

Shortly after Rayburn became the majority leader of the 75th Congress, Roosevelt asked him to come to the White House for a conference. The matter the President wanted to discuss was a plan for adding more justices to the Supreme Court. Most of the judges were Republicans who had been appointed under Presidents Harding, Coolidge, and Hoover; and many of them had already reached the retirement age. President Roosevelt felt that if these justices wished to continue working, it was perfectly all right; but that a new justice should be added anyway when one of the older members of the Court reached 70 years of age. To many Democrats, Roosevelt's plan seemed reasonable enough. But to others it looked like an attempt by the President to "pack" the Supreme Court of the country with men who would always approve his measures. Sam Rayburn shared this latter feeling.

Under the Constitution, the government is divided into three branches: executive, legislative, and judicial. None should have unchecked power over the other two—and Sam Rayburn agreed entirely with this principle. He had personally chosen the legislative branch for his own career, but he did not believe the Congress should be superior to the Presidency or to the Supreme Court. By the same token, he did not think the President should have power over the Court.

But it was the majority leader's duty to try to get the Roosevelt bill into Congress for its consideration. The idea of putting in new judges before old ones were retired met with all the opposition Rayburn predicted. Finally, Rayburn and several other key Democrats, including Vice President Garner, convinced President Roosevelt that the plan would never pass Congress. The President agreed reluctantly to let the plan drop. The decision proved to be a wise one; for during his years in the White House, the President made his full share of appointments to the Supreme Court, seven between 1937 and 1941.

Later in 1937, Rayburn was able to take a vacation, returning to his Fannin County farm between sessions of Congress. It was a pleasant change from his life as majority leader, which required not only the extra duties of the job itself, but even more speechmaking than usual around the country. Before Rayburn left for his home in Texas, he made important speeches at Harvard University on how a bill passes Congress and at Arlington Cemetery near Washington for the Confederate Memorial Day Services. More than ever that year, he appreciated the quiet of his home, his good friends around Bonham and the District, and, of course, the big Rayburn family.

He spent happy days during the summer, not even having to worry about the Democratic primary, still a year away. Instead, he concentrated on improving the farm. He bought 900 more acres in the northern part of Fannin County and announced that in the future the Rayburns would switch from raising dairy cattle to beef cattle. At that time, Rayburn's change to beef cattle was revolutionary in his part of North Texas. Mostly, the crops were cotton and corn, and the livestock was either dairy cattle or hogs, with most of the emphasis on what is known in Texas as "King Cotton." Rayburn's move to beef cattle was among the first. Until that time, raising beef was restricted to southern and western parts of the state. But within a few years, such pioneers as Rayburn proved to others in the area that there was more profit in raising beef, thus changing the agricultural economy of the entire section. North and East Texas is now as much a ranching country as the vast stretches of land to the west and south.

In the following year, 1938, Mr. Democrat had one of his most successful years in Congress. He had returned to Washington refreshed by his short vacation, happy with the plans for the new 900 acres, and eager to get to work on a good legislative program to help his own Fourth District. By midyear Congress approved his bill for a $54,000,000 project later called the Denison Dam. A huge dam constructed on the Red River, it created the largest man-made lake in the United States at the time. It also provided irrigation and flood control, as well as a tremendous source of power for both Texas and Oklahoma. Soon after the bill was passed, people in the Fourth began urging Congress to name the project Rayburn Dam. But Mr. Democrat refused, feeling the choice of name might not be welcomed in Oklahoma. He suggested a name that would refer to the region, such as Denison or, perhaps, Texoma—

combining the words *Texas* and *Oklahoma*. The final decision was to name the dam Denison and the lake it created Texoma.

The victory with his dam project was followed quickly by the Democratic primary election in the Fourth District, and for one of the few times in his career, Sam Rayburn was unopposed. With business growing better each year and with such projects as the Denison Dam adding to the welfare of the area, no one could summon the courage to run against the majority leader of the House. The entire population of the Fourth District seemed to approve of Sam Rayburn's conduct in Washington. And perhaps they were a little in awe—or even disbelief—that one of their own was actually majority leader.

In the following months—as the 75th Congress ended and the 76th began in 1939—his attention slowly shifted. Many of the severe problems of the Depression were being solved, but they were replaced by more problems from outside the nation. Once again, war clouds were gathering over Europe.

In 1933, Germany had withdrawn from the League of Nations. Two years later, Italy invaded Ethiopia in defiance of the League. Within a year, Italy and Germany formed a Rome-Berlin "Axis," which soon defied not only the League of Nations but the world itself. While the war-storm was still on the European horizon, even more trouble arose in Asia as Japan withdrew from the League of Nations and invaded China in 1937. By the spring of 1938, German Dictator Adolf Hitler took over Austria. A few months later, the British and French governments agreed to Hitler's taking a part of Czechoslovakia.

Meanwhile, in the Congress of the United States, Sam Rayburn was determined not to be caught napping as the nation had been just before World War I. Rayburn gave each bill that was presented to strengthen America's position the full support and influence of his position as the majority leader of the

House. On the Naval Authorization Bill, Rayburn voted to increase the number of aircraft carriers, submarines, destroyers, and cruisers. Later, he fought hard in the Congress for military aid to China. Many of the isolationists claimed that it would be immoral for the United States government to give arms and ammunition to China in its fight against Japan. In reply to these critics, Rayburn fired back: "When great governments, with ambitious men who have a desire to control the earth, attempt to stamp out liberty and democracy, is there any immorality in supplying arms to a little weak country so that it may let the dictators . . . of the earth know that it can . . . get arms to protect its liberty?"

The mistake of trusting Adolf Hitler's word was soon apparent. Hitler moved again, this time taking over all of Czechoslovakia. By the end of summer in 1939, Germany and the Soviet Union agreed to a nonaggression pact. Hitler began his famed "blitzkrieg" on Poland on September 1, 1939, and the world was swept into the beginning of World War II. Both France and England were committed to defending Poland's independence, and entered the war against Germany.

As the people of the United States grew increasingly concerned, Sam Rayburn became one of the great spokesmen in Washington for having a strong, armed United States fighting force. For the second time the man from Fannin County witnessed a war in Europe slowly begin to pull the United States into conflict. This time, Rayburn insisted, the nation must be ready.

As 1940 began, Sam Rayburn looked forward to what he expected might be the most serious and hardest of his years in Congress. With grim determination he returned to Washington after the Christmas holidays, ready to ride out the coming storm as the majority leader.

Chapter 12

Speaker of the House

In addition to the war in Europe and Japan's increasing conquests in Asia, Rayburn looked forward to other events that would shape the future. For his own part, another election loomed in the summer in the Fourth District of Texas. Too, there would be the national political conventions and, in the fall, the election of a President.

The Republicans were insisting that the Democratic administration of President Roosevelt and the Democratic leadership in Congress were dragging the nation into the European war. To these charges, Rayburn answered, "The Democratic Party at this time is not the war Party, it will not be the war Party, but it intends to be, wishes to be, and it will be the Party for the defense of America and its great institutions."

Looking to the coming national convention, Rayburn made his position clear: he once more would support John Garner for the Democratic nomination. But to his surprise, Rayburn's own name was being mentioned as a possible nom-

Chairmen of the Texas delegation Rayburn planned the Garner campaign with organizer E. B. Germany at Chicago headquarters.

[106]

inee! This talk, however, did not impress the man from Fannin County; for he realized there was no true organization behind him, and he knew this was necessary to win. At the same time, there was a strong feeling President Roosevelt might break with tradition and seek a third term. So many people in the Democratic party were against a third term that the President himself refused to make an announcement, but there was really almost no doubt in anyone's mind. Garner and Rayburn took, then, a position against Roosevelt in their decision to try to gain the nomination for Garner. For them both, it proved to be an important decision.

By April 1, still another surprise appeared. The Speaker of the House, William Bankhead, had been in poor health and was finally hospitalized. The great chair on the rostrum of the House of Representatives was empty! To fill it while the Speaker was ill, the House named its majority leader, Sam Rayburn of Texas, as Speaker *pro tempore*. For the first time in its history, Washington heard the loud and decisive blow of Sam Rayburn's gavel in the halls of Congress. It was a sound the members of the House would not soon forget, for the Rayburn gavel technique was not to rap a quick sequence, but to bring the gavel down hard and fast in a single crack of the wood that could not fail to bring the attention of every member to the Chair. As the members looked at the temporary Speaker, his face kept its same sternness, but from the Chair his appearance was somehow different. He looked as if he "belonged" there. The trademark of his baldness was complete by 1940, and it added to this impressive mien.

When summer came, Rayburn ignored his opposition in the Fourth District. Congress was still in session and world conditions were far too serious for him to consider leaving Washington for a political campaign. Apparently, the people of the

Fourth felt his decision was right, for they gave him an over-whelming victory with almost 40,000 votes. During the same month, July, the Democratic convention began in Chicago.

In many ways, it was a strange convention. Roosevelt sent a message to be read to the delegates, stating that he would not seek a third term. Still, when names were put in nomination, Franklin Roosevelt's was among them. John Garner was the other nominee for President. At the end of the roll call, the Roosevelt delegates ignored the President's message and voted for him anyway. Garner received only 61 votes, and many wondered at the sincerity of Roosevelt's statement. With the decision of the convention made, Sam Rayburn moved to the platform with a suggestion that Roosevelt's nomination be made unanimous. Even though Rayburn deeply wanted to have the nomination for his old friend, Jack Garner, it was obviously a hopeless situation. His motion to have Roosevelt's nomination a unanimous choice helped to bring the party together—and should have indicated to Franklin Roosevelt his and Garner's basic friendliness and support. Unfortunately, it did not.

President Roosevelt's attitude toward the two Texans was reflected in the convention's nomination of a candidate for vice president. Garner had been openly opposed to a third term by any man, including President Roosevelt. Garner felt much the same way about the vice presidency, and gave no indication that he would like to continue in that post. On the contrary, he indicated he would prefer to return to his home in Uvalde, Tex-as, and make a permanent departure from the "boiling sea of politics." Rayburn then became a logical and natural choice for the vice presidential nomination.

When his name was seriously mentioned for the nomina-tion, Rayburn was quite naturally interested. The feel of Speak-er Bankhead's gavel, however, reminded him of his old ambition to hold the highest office in the Congress of the United States. So, while the vice presidency was a high honor, it was also a tremendous change from the legislative to the executive branch of government. Rayburn in 1940 had slightly mixed emotions about the opportunity. He perhaps even welcomed the fact that still another Texas candidate was being talked about as the nominee, Jesse Jones of Houston. As head of the Reconstruction Finance Corporation and publisher of the Houston *Chronicle,* Jones would have been an outstanding candidate. But he was more a publisher and a businessman than he was a politician, and he decided he would rather have the Texas delegation vote for Sam Rayburn than for himself. Just as the Texans decided to back Rayburn, however, Jones received word that President Roosevelt's personal choice for a running mate was Secretary of Agriculture Henry A. Wallace.

Immediately, Sam Rayburn requested that the Texas delegation not put his name before the convention, but instead give its votes to the President's choice. The majority of the Texas delegation did not approve of Roosevelt's selecting Wallace over Rayburn; and when the convention began balloting, Texas gave its support to Speaker Bankhead for vice president. Bankhead, in fact, could have won if Rayburn had not decided to support the President's choice. Rayburn could have left his own name in nomination and held the support of all the Garner people in the convention. Along with Bankhead's supporters, this would have been sufficient to block Wallace. After the convention had been deadlocked, Rayburn could then have switched his votes to Bankhead and defeated Wallace with ease. And—with Bankhead moving out of Congress—Rayburn would have been assured of becoming Speaker.

Politicians are trained by experience to take advantage of every opportunity—and Sam Rayburn was a master politician.

[109]

Still, he ignored the great chance to prove his power over the President's personal selection and to become, in the process, the Speaker of the House of Representatives. In terms of logic, it is difficult to explain Mr. Democrat's action in supporting Wallace at the 1940 convention. But if logic fails to explain Sam Rayburn, an understanding of the man himself does not. Sam Rayburn was a man who was able to take the longer view of history. He did not forget his ambition to become the Speaker, but he was not so ambitious that he wanted to tear apart his own political party to gain a simple, personal victory. Even President Roosevelt realized the importance of Rayburn's decision, for the President telephoned Rayburn to thank him personally for his unselfish support in the convention. Roosevelt, too, could take the longer view of things. He knew Sam Rayburn could be of great value in the future.

The Republican convention selected an outstanding candidate in Wendell L. Willkie. As the president of a large corporation, Willkie appealed to the businessmen of the country. At the same time he was not opposed to a vigorous federal government that could cope with the problems of world leadership. Willkie had, in fact, been a Democrat until a short time before the 1940 Republican convention. The vice presidential nominee was Senator Charles McNary of Oregon. This gave the Republicans a wide appeal to farmers through McNary and to businessmen through Willkie. It was by far the strongest ticket the Republicans had come up with since their nomination of Herbert Hoover in 1928. Willkie, a political dark horse, campaigned hard, and Rayburn began to wonder if the tall Midwesterner might pull off an upset victory.

Sam Rayburn looked forward to the election with growing concern that Roosevelt might lose. In Congress, the man from Fannin County continued his work as the majority leader under Speaker Bankhead. It was now a familiar routine, one which Rayburn expected would continue for several more years, provided the Democrats kept their House majority.

But suddenly, the pattern was broken in September, 1940. Speaker Bankhead became seriously ill and within a few days was dead. Two days later, on September 16, the House of Representatives met to select Bankhead's successor. John McCormack of Massachusetts introduced the simple resolution that Mr. Democrat himself—Sam Rayburn of Texas—be elected to the office. The voice vote of the House was unanimous.

Even though it was the crowning moment of Sam Rayburn's career as a United States Congressman, it was an occassion filled at the same time with sadness. Speaker Bankhead had been one of the most distinguished and best liked men in Congress. At the state funeral held in the House, the new Speaker stated his feelings for Bankhead: "For 25 years or more I was given a rich friendship which I will remember to my last days. It was given to me by a great statesman, by a great man with a great soul. The House has lost a great man. Will Bankhead was a human being. He loved people *en masse*. His was a great soul."

At home in the Fourth District, the news that their Congressman had been elected to the highest office in the Congress blazed in the headlines. Giant homecoming celebrations were planned to honor the new Speaker in October. After 27 years of service in the House, Rayburn was honored with the biggest parade Bonham had ever seen. Eleven bands joined with beautifully decorated floats in the mile-long parade, led by Mr. Democrat himself through the crowded downtown streets, as thousands cheered their welcome to Fannin County's greatest citizen, their own "Mr. Sam."

It was a day Sam Rayburn would never forget.

Chapter 13

Preparing for War

I n the national election of 1940, Wendell Willkie lost, but he still managed to win almost 45 percent of the popular vote. In the House and in the Senate, the Democrats rolled up even larger majorities than they had held in the 76th Congress. Such an extension of Democratic candidates' popularity would normaly point to an extension of Democratic votes for Roosevelt. But many of the people were opposed to any President being given a third term, and they voted for Willkie.

On January 2, 1941, the Democrats of the new 77th Congress met for the first time. It took them only a few minutes to select Speaker Rayburn for a full term in his new position as the leader of the legislative branch of the government. As his gavel banged the Congress into session, Sam Rayburn entered a new era of his already distinguished career in government.

In the following months, the world situation continued to worsen. France already had fallen to the Germans, and Hitler pushed the British into the sea and out of France at Dunkirk.

Speaker Rayburn and Rep. Clifford A. Woodrum (Dem., Va.) studied Roosevelt's $7,000,000,000 defense appropriation request, 1941.

The German *Luftwaffe* continued bombing England, and the people of the United States watched with great concern and wondered how long the British could last.

Even though Americans everywhere sympathized with the British, there was still a large group opposed to any American aid. These isolationists had the same attitude that defeated Woodrow Wilson's great plan for United States membership in the League of Nations. Now—in 1941—the same sort of thinking caused some members of the Congress to oppose the president's "Lend-Lease" program of assistance to such nations as Britain and China. Fiercely, Rayburn fought those who wanted to ignore America's friends in Europe. Speaking on a national radio network, the new Speaker of the House reminded his fellow Americans: "Let us awake. Let us defend America

[113]

now. Let us give Britain the support necessary to hold Hitler at bay and to keep war from America."

The Speaker won his battle, as the House approved the Lend-Lease bill on February 8, 1941. It passed the Senate on March 8 and was signed into law on March 11 by President Roosevelt. It was a good victory for Rayburn and other lawmakers who realized the importance of the Lend-Lease program. But it was only a warm-up for the legislative battle that lay just ahead. August 12, 1941, loomed as a tremendously important date for the Congress and for the people of the United States of America.

The Selective Service Act was about to expire. If it were not extended, the army of the United States would shrink to a mere 400,000 men. And, with the international situation so dangerous, a small army would be an open invitation for Hitler to attack America itself. Still, there was a strong group in the House that wanted to let the Act expire. People "back home" were writing their Congressmen, urging them not to renew the Act. Many legislators in the House were afraid they would be voted out of office if they went against the desires of their constituents. Rayburn, of course, was sympathetic with these problems of Congressmen; but he pointed out that the future of the nation depended on their vote to extend Selective Service and thus keep a reasonably large American fighting force. Rayburn's belief was backed up by the Chiefs of Staff and by President Roosevelt. And it was to Sam Rayburn these men looked for the leadership that would keep the United States strong enough to fight off an invader from Europe or Asia.

When the day for voting finally arrived and the roll call began, Speaker Rayburn stood silently by the Clerk's side, watching as each Congressman's vote was recorded. Not since the dark days of the Civil War had there been such tension in the Great House. Rayburn watched, keeping his own record, as the 435 names were called upon to vote. A total of 405 votes were cast. Rayburn made the announcement immediately.

"On this vote," Rayburn said slowly, "203 members have voted 'Aye,' 202 members have voted 'No' and the bill is passed."

Congressman Short of Missouri requested a recount in order to be certain that the Rayburn forces had won. As the recount was being made—and with no errors being found—the next step for the opponents of Selective Service would be to make a motion for reconsideration. A Congressman cannot change his vote once it is announced, but if a bill is put under reconsideration, a new vote is necessary. As the recount went on for several minutes, it became obvious no error would be found, and that reconsideration was the only hope for Rayburn's opponents in the House. They planned to make this motion as soon as the recount was completed.

At the end of the recount, Sam Rayburn struck with lightning speed. "No correction in the vote, the vote stands, and the bill is passed—" Then, without even pausing for breath, Rayburn ripped on with a stroke of legislative genius, ". . . and without objection a motion to reconsider is laid on the table." The Speaker looked across the members of the House and *not one* realized that the Speaker was only a gavel-stroke away from victory. The key was in Mr. Democrat's statement that *without objection,* all motions to reconsider the Selective Service Act would be *laid on the table,* a parliamentary phrase meaning— in a word—ended. If no member raised an objection, the opportunity to reconsider would be gone.

From his seat on the rostrum, the Speaker waited for a moment, then brought the heavy gavel down hard. The bill was *passed!*

Stunned, the opponents of the bill finally came to life. Congressman Short even made a motion for reconsideration, but Rayburn pointed out that his opportunity had already gone by for such a motion. Another Congressman, Andersen of Minnesota, could not believe that Rayburn had struck his side down so easily. "I beg to differ with the Speaker," Andersen said. "The Speaker did not announce that a motion to reconsider had been tabled."

"The Chair has twice stated that he did make that statement," Rayburn said.

"I beg to differ with you," Andersen began once more. But Rayburn interrupted, beginning now to be annoyed.

"The Chair does not intend to have his word questioned by the gentleman from Minnesota or anybody else!"

That was the end of the discussion. Sam Rayburn had hammered through a great victory in Congress. From the standpoint of parliamentary genius, he proved to every member in the House that no other Speaker in the long history of the nation was his superior. His victory in extending the Selective Service Act continues to stand as one of Mr. Democrat's greatest achievements. It was much more than a mere personal victory, for it provided the United States with an army of 1,500,-000 men when the United States entered World War II. Had Rayburn failed to push the bill through the House, the United States would have had a pathetic army of under 500,000 at the time Pearl Harbor was attacked.

In the weeks that followed, President Roosevelt realized the full value of Rayburn's accomplishment. The United States government's relations with both Germany and Japan were growing worse with each passing day. By October 1941, the Germans attacked and sank the U. S. destroyer *Reuben James* with the loss of 76 lives. Immediately, President Roosevelt ordered the Navy to shoot on sight any German submarine found in American defense waters. Japan had signed a pact with the Axis nations, Germany and Italy. Hitler had broken his nonaggression agreement with the Soviet Union in June of 1941, and the United States promply had begun helping the Russians under the Lend-Lease program.

Two days after Sam Rayburn's victory in keeping an adequate number of men in the United States Army through Selective Service, Franklin Roosevelt and Winston Churchill met at sea, in the North Atlantic Ocean in a series of secret sessions. Known as the Atlantic Charter, their agreement outlined the British and American positions and intentions in fighting the war and explained what postwar policies would be.

Troubles with Japan were deepening. The Japanese general, Tojo, who became premier in October 1941, sent a special envoy to the United States, Saburo Kurusu, whose announced purpose was to keep the peace between Japan and America. Kurusu joined the Japanese ambassador, Admiral Kichisaburo Nomura, and a series of visits began with the American Secretary of State, Cordell Hull. The Japanese representatives demanded that America recognize Japan's conquest of China, and stop giving the Chinese aid through the Lend-Lease program. Hull, meanwhile, was insisting that Japan withdraw from the Axis, remove its troops from China and French Indo-China, and further agree to stop its acts of war. Talks continued into early December, but it was apparent the two governments would not be able to reach an agreement. On Saturday, December 6, President Roosevelt sent a message to Emperor Hirohito, the supreme leader of the Japanese people, asking for his cooperation. But the next day, Japan's answer came as its air force struck in a surprise attack on Pearl Harbor, the United States Navy's huge base in Hawaii.

The result was a tragic loss of lives and equipment for the United States. Eight battleships and ten smaller ships were sunk or severely damaged and almost 250 aircraft were destroyed or damaged. The loss of American lives was staggering; over 3,000 persons were killed or missing. Including injuries, the number totaled over 4,500 casualties.

President Roosevelt acted swiftly, asking for a special joint session of both houses of Congress the next day, Monday, December 8. Sam Rayburn remembered well the time President Wilson had come to Congress on a similar mission, asking Congress to declare war on Germany. This time, the scene looked different, for Rayburn now sat on the high rostrum as the Speaker behind President Roosevelt. Solemnly, Rayburn listened as President Roosevelt's powerful and moving voice described December 7, 1941, as "a date which will live in infamy."

Four hours after Roosevelt's brief speech, Sam Rayburn's gavel echoed the nation's determination as the Congress committed the United States to a state of war with Japan. On December 11, Germany moved to Japan's side with a declaration of war on the United States. On the same day, Rayburn's gavel answered as Congress returned Germany's declaration with its own.

The flashbulbs of the press cameras went off brightly as the Speaker of the House put his signature on the Joint Resolution that declared the war. When the photographs appeared in the newspapers around the country, they had caught the grimness of the Speaker's face, the determination that could be seen from Tokyo to Berlin. It was not just Mr. Sam of Bonham whose penstroke was photographed. It was the face, as well, of an angered and determined America.

Chapter 14

War Again

The United States forces reeled back in the early days of the war with Japan, for the attack on Pearl Harbor had cut deeply into United States' strength. American Marines at Wake Island in the Pacific held out valiantly but were finally defeated. In the Philippine Islands, the Japanese poured in a strong invasion force, soon taking the important city of Manila and Cavite naval base. Early in January 1942, General Douglas MacArthur was forced to retreat, and then began his masterful defense of the Bataan Peninsula. By March, MacArthur was ordered to Australia to assume command of the Allied forces in the Southwest Pacific. General Jonathan N. Wainwright, who replaced him on Bataan, finally was forced to surrender in May.

By June, Japan had taken Hong Kong, Singapore, Burma, Malaya, and most of the East Indies, and was threatening to move on India and even Australia. For the first time, it occurred to the American people that they might actually lose

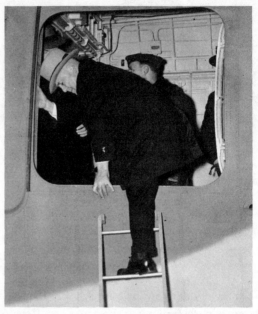

Speaker Rayburn climbed out of a PBM-3 bomber during a Congressional tour

the war to Japan. In Washington, Speaker Rayburn announced he would not tolerate any "dilly-dallying" by the House in acting on important war legislation.

An example of Rayburn's attitude toward getting things done quickly to help the war effort was his handling of a cut in the draft age. The Selective Service Act did not allow 18 and 19 year old men to be drafted into the armed forces. But, with the war not going well, the need to increase the nation's military strength was apparent. When the Speaker announced his intentions to get a bill passed that would allow drafting younger men, letters poured in from every state. Most of them violently opposed drafting men so young. It appeared Rayburn might be in for another battle to equal his first one with the extension of the Selective Service Act in 1941. But just before

[120]

the bill was to be voted on by the House, Rayburn came up with an unusual and brilliant idea to get the bill passed. The Speaker contacted President Roosevelt and arranged to have the Army Chief of Staff, General George Marshall, and Secretary of War Henry L. Stimson, talk with individual members' of Congress. After these leaders explained the importance of extending Selective Service to include men 18 and 19 years old, Rayburn felt confident the bill would pass much more easily. He was right. The bill went through, and Sam Rayburn once more received the congratulations of such men as Roosevelt, Stimson, and Marshall.

The war raged on in the Pacific, and in Europe Hitler was winning victory after victory, having taken Rumania, Hungary, Bulgaria, and Greece. Hitler then moved against the Soviet Union until he threatened to take the important city of Stalingrad. Britain and the United States agreed to open a second battleground to draw some of Hitler's army away from the Soviets.

With such tension in the world, Sam Rayburn scarcely noticed that 1942 was another election year in the Fourth District of Texas. A man named George Balch of Commerce, where Rayburn had attended Mayo College, announced he would run against the Speaker. Rayburn ignored his opponent and attended to the more important matters in Washington. Balch campaigned hard and was defeated by 25,000 votes for his trouble. The election gave a 16th term to Fannin County's famous Mr. Sam.

Of more importance to Rayburn in 1942 was the general situation of politics throughout the state of Texas. An extremely colorful character, W. Lee O'Daniel, had arrived on the Texas political scene in 1938. With a hillbilly band, "The Lightcrust Doughboys," he managed to get elected governor.

O'Daniel seemed to be against everything. He hated big business and he hated labor. He was against such Democrats as Rayburn, Garner, and Roosevelt. He disliked Republicans such as Hoover and Willkie. The only positive idea he seemed to have was his affection for making speeches and playing old-fashioned hillbilly music! It was one of those unhappy turns of history, but the voters of Texas loved him.

Ridiculous though the new governor of Texas was to many people, O'Daniel's rise in Texas politics caused a major split in the Democratic party in the state—and this was not amusing to Rayburn. A little later United States Senator Morris Sheppard died, and O'Daniel announced he would be a candidate to fill out the rest of the term. One of the opposing candidates was Congressman Lyndon B. Johnson, who lost to O'Daniel by the narrow margin of 111 votes.

In Washington, Speaker Rayburn found Senator O'Daniel to be much more troublesome than he had been in Austin, perhaps for the simple reason that O'Daniel was so much nearer. Among other things, O'Daniel was opposed to Selective Service, without which America would have lost the war. He was also violent in his criticism of the President and of Rayburn's leadership of the Congress. His fight against labor unions and against paying overtime wages to workers was equally vigorous. When he returned to Texas in 1942 to run for a full, six-year term in the Senate, he pointed proudly to the fact that he had been overwhelmingly defeated on every issue he had fought for.

Mostly, O'Daniel appealed to the extreme conservatives in Texas, along with many of the rural voters. Rayburn did what he could to help Governor James Allred in the election, but O'Daniel won again and was given a six-year term in the Senate that would last until 1948. The most important feature of O'Daniel's election was the split among Texas Democrats, a troublesome fact that was to become one of the more severe problems Sam Rayburn had in his home state.

Sam Rayburn returned to Washington for the opening of the 78th Congress early in 1943. During the month of political activity in Texas, the war effort of the United States had improved steadily. In the Pacific, an attack by the Japanese on Midway Island was thrown back. American forces moved into the Solomon Islands.

A "second front" was opened when a combined British-American force invaded Africa and won control of Morocco and Algeria. In the fall of 1942, Hitler had been forced to send troops from Europe to meet the attack in Africa. With the snows of winter, the Russians struck back in a massive attack. As 1943 began, the Royal Air Force was joined by the United States Air Force in a tremendous air assault on Germany. At last the great industrial strength of the United States was beginning to break down the Axis' power all over the world.

In Washington, Rayburn was elected to another term as Speaker. His efforts to push important war-effort bills through the complicated machinery of the House was recognized as an outstanding contribution to the Allied success. Many persons —including Axis leaders—believed the government of the United States was too awkward to move quickly. They felt the Democrats and Republicans in Congress would argue among themselves until disaster struck. But these people were wrong, for under the leadership of Rayburn, the Congress acted promptly and efficiently.

One recognition of Rayburn's World War II leadership was the unveiling of his portrait in the Texas Legislature in Austin on April 27, 1943. Still another came on August 6, when his college—now East Texas State—conferred on him a

[123]

Doctor of Law degree. But the greatest honor came later in the year as newspaper editorials began to mention "Mr. Sam" as an excellent choice for the Presidential nomination in 1944. These articles pleased Rayburn, but he did not take them very seriously. President Roosevelt had already broken the tradition of only two terms in the White House. To Rayburn, it seemed likely Roosevelt would run for a fourth term in 1944. The rumors, however, that Rayburn might become Roosevelt's running mate as the vice presidential nominee did make sense.

At the start of 1944, Rayburn was being mentioned more and more for the vice presidency. As a Southwesterner, the Speaker would have been a pleasing candidate to the Southern states. And many of the President's advisers felt Rayburn's presence on the ticket would increase the Democrats' chances to win the White House once more. There were, however, other names being mentioned for vice president, including that of Senator Harry S. Truman of Missouri. His chief claim to national recognition had come from his committee to investigate national defense.

In the spring, Sam Rayburn made his decision. At least, he made *part* of a decision: to present some of his views of the United States to the people of the nation. He made great speeches in both Los Angeles and in San Francisco. Rayburn spoke with affection about men in the United States "of all political views" and how their faith in the nation had brought them together. He described this faith—shared by both Democrats and Republicans—as being above personal interest or personal political affiilations. These were not political speeches; they were, instead, thoughts from the heart of the Speaker of the House.

These moments of greatness for the man from Fannin County were followed soon by a defeat dealt to him by a handful of his fellow Texans. In an amazing show of treachery, Texas lost its best chance to have one of its great men in the White House.

The same spirit that had moved W. Lee O'Daniel into the governor's mansion in Austin had also attracted other Texas politicians, many of them superior to O'Daniel, but all just as critical of Roosevelt's program of liberal legislation. They formed an organization called the "Texas Regulars," which succeeded in taking over the Democratic party in the state. And, since they were opposed to Roosevelt, they also attacked Sam Rayburn at the moment he was beginning a certain rise to the vice presidential nomination. Governor Coke Stevenson led the group that decided to refuse to endorse Rayburn in the coming national convention. Many of these Texas Regular conservatives finally came to the discovery that they were not Democrats after all, and they became important organizers of the Republican party in the state. For Rayburn's part, it was unfortunate these men did not get out of the Democratic party before the 1944 campaign.

But they did not; instead, they took the position that Sam Rayburn was already too big, too powerful. Along with their decision to block Rayburn as the vice presidential nominee, they also decided to make an all-out effort to defeat the Speaker in his own Fourth District! And, as the national convention came near in the summer, Rayburn was unable to attend. Instead, he was fighting for his political life in the Fourth against two opponents.

In making the race for his 17th term in Congress, Rayburn made an important decision. Many felt he could have gone to the Democratic national convention and fought to victory, even without the backing of the Texas delegation. Few professional politicians paid attention to the Coke Stevenson group, anyway.

Most of the delegates realized the party in Texas was being controlled by a group that did not represent the feelings of the people. In 1944, Sam Rayburn was by far the most popular man in Texas, and Governor Stevenson would not have wanted his own popularity tested at the polls against the Speaker. Still, Rayburn ignored the opportunity to go to the Chicago convention and fight for the nomination. After weighing the possibilities in his own mind, he decided once more that the House of Representatives was his home.

When the votes were in, the money spent to defeat the Speaker had been wasted. Rayburn pulled 22,052 votes, State Senator G. C. Morris received 16,705, and George Balch got 816. At the Democratic convention, Roosevelt took the position that he preferred to have the powerful Rayburn in control of Congress. With his recommendation, the convention nominated Rayburn's good friend, Harry Truman.

The Republican Party, meanwhile, was having its own troubles in selecting candidates. Wendell Willkie decided he did not have enough strength to win the nomination a second time. Instead, he threw his votes to prevent the nomination of one of the party's isolationists who might block America's participation in a new world organization, such as the United Nations became. The Republicans finally nominated Thomas E. Dewey after a struggle with Ohio Senator Robert Taft, an extremely conservative Republican. In the election, Roosevelt won his fourth term in office, defeating Dewey by over 3,000,-000 votes. The Democrats gained 21 additional seats in the House of Representatives, assuring Sam Rayburn of another two year term as the Speaker.

During the political conventions and the months that followed, the war in Europe and in the Pacific continued to go in favor of the Allies, a fact that doubtless helped Franklin

Roosevelt continue his long residence in the White House. In June of 1944, the Allies' Supreme Commander Dwight Eisenhower led his forces across the English Channel in a direct invastion of Hitler's "Fortress Europe." Within 12 weeks, the Allied force had conquered Normandy and pushed forward to liberate Paris from the Germans. By late August, the Allied army invaded France from the Mediterranean, and destroyed the Seventh German Army.

In the Pacific, General MacArthur kept his promise to "return" by invading Leyte Island in the Philippines on October 20, 1944. With the beginning of the new year, the city of Manila was captured, and the liberation of the Philippines was assured. In February, the Americans won Iwo Jima. By the first of April, Okinawa fell to the Americans. The Japanese were fighting only a defensive war and victory was in sight.

As the 79th Congress opened, Sam Rayburn looked forward eagerly to the peace that would come. He also glanced back over the years he had been in the House. "I love this life," the Speaker said. "It has been my life for nearly 32 years. Next to home and family and friends, it is my love." The man from Fannin County was 63 years old in 1945, and he was approaching new records for his long service as a Congressman and even as a Speaker. The simple name "Mr. Sam" was a tribute in its simplicity for the Speaker of the House. He sat in the great chair, high above the floor of the House, with the soft illumination from the skylight on his solemn face.

He looked at his fellow Congressmen with the sad eyes that still could penetrate so deeply that often it was confused as sternness. The vice presidency was not his, but by his hand was the most powerful gavel in the world. It took its great strength from the firm hand that held its long handle. This fact, even the Texas Regulars could not deny.

[127]

Chapter **15**

In The Minority Again

T he spring of 1945 brought victory in the European war; but before the final surrender on May 7, the nation was stunned by the death on April 12 of President Roosevelt.

In the weeks before the death of the President, Sam Rayburn had known that he was not well. After he went to Warm Springs, Georgia, for a rest, Rayburn decided he should have a talk with his close friend, Vice President Harry Truman. Rayburn correctly read the future, and he wanted Truman to be prepared if something happened to the President. On the morning of April 12, the Speaker called his friend and suggested a meeting. It was a day Sam Rayburn would never forget. Several years later, Rayburn recalled what happened for C. Dwight Dorough, who put it in his excellent book, *Mr. Sam:*

"On April 12 I phoned him. I said, 'Harry, why don't we have a little meeting?' Well, there were three or four or five fellows in the office. Lew Deschler, the parliamentarian of the House was there, and I think Bill White of the New York *Times* was there, and one or two more. And he [Truman] says, 'All right, I'll come over.' And I went to the office which they used to call the Bureau of Education. . . . in just a few minutes, why the telephone rang, and they said, 'Is the Vice-President there?' And they said, 'Tell him to call the White House, Mr. Early at the White House, as quickly as possible.'

"Well, Truman came in, and I said, 'Harry, they said for you to call the White House.'

"Well, he said he didn't know what it was about. Roosevelt was at Warm Springs. He thought he might have come back suddenly and wanted to see him, or something like that.

"And he picked up the telephone and he said, 'This is the VP, and Mr. Early wants to talk to me.' And he [Early] talked. He [Truman] is kind of a pale fellow anyhow and he got a little paler, and he hung up the telephone, and he said, 'Steve Early has asked me to come to the White House as quickly as possible and as quietly as possible.'

"And he left. I think he went out and caught a taxi and went to the White House, as well as I remember. [Mr. Truman states that Tom Harty, his chauffeur, drove him to the Pennsylvania Avenue entrance without the Secret Service guard, whom they had eluded. The time was 5:25 P. M.]

"In a few minutes we got a flash that the President was dead. And then in a little while we had a call to come down to the White House, which I knew was to see Truman sworn in."

At 7:09 P.M., Sam Rayburn was one of a few important men who watched as Chief Justice Harlan Stone swore in Harry S. Truman as the new President. The New Deal of Roosevelt was ended, and the Fair Deal of Truman had begun.

Saddened though he was by Franklin Roosevelt's death, Mr. Sam had full confidence in the ability of his friend from Missouri. Rayburn wrote soon after Roosevelt's death: "President Roosevelt's passing will shock and sadden good people everywhere. The American Nation has been well led in every crisis. In Harry Truman we have a leader in whom I have complete confidence."

The new President, however, received help on several occasions from the more experienced Speaker. One of the most famous incidents came only a few days after the new President entered office. On April 16, 1945, President Truman was scheduled to make his first major speech before the two houses of Congress. When he was escorted to the rostrum of the House of Representatives, he was quite naturally nervous and as soon as he arrived near the microphones, he began his speech without even an introduction from his official host, the Speaker.

Quickly, Sam Rayburn leaned forward and whispered, "Just a moment—let me present you, Harry, will you?"

The President paused, realizing his mistake. For the Congress of the United States is; in itself, equal in power to the Presidency. Truman was the official guest of his full political equal, represented in the two houses of Congress. It would have been more than "impolite" for Truman to have spoken without an introduction. But Rayburn covered quickly for him.

With simple dignity, Sam Rayburn announced: "The President of the United States." He then moved to his own large Speaker's chair.

In less than a month, President Truman announced that the Germans had surrendered. For his part, the Speaker released a statement to the press: "With all Americans . . . I rejoice in the signal victory achieved by the American and other Allied armies over the hordes of Hitler. It is my fervent wish that this may shorten the war all over the world."

By mid summer of 1945, President Truman had reached a difficult decision. He asked the Japanese to make an unconditional surrender or face total destruction. When they did not surrender, he authorized the use of the atomic bomb on Hiroshima on August 5 and on Nagasaki three days later. Immediately, the Japanese realized they would be bombed off the face of the earth if they continued the war. They appealed for peace. The war in the Pacific was ended on August 14, 1945. Horrible though the destruction was, Truman's order to use the atomic bomb brought the war to a quick end and saved thousands of lives. Throughout the making of the Truman decision, Sam Rayburn was kept informed.

The joy the Speaker felt over the ending of World War II was followed within a few days by a minor annoyance. While working with some of his cattle on his Fannin County ranch, Rayburn stumbled over some old bedsprings that had been thrown away in the tall grass and broke his left arm. A friend was with him; so he was driven quickly to a nearby hospital to have his arm set. Later, President Truman called from Washington and Rayburn assured him there was nothing to worry about. It would be simply a matter of time until the Speaker would be able to get back to work. Meanwhile, the broken arm kept him inside his home west of Bonham, and he was able to visit longer and more often with his friends.

It was fortunate that Rayburn did find some time for rest in 1945, for the next year brought an avalanche of political troubles to the Democratic party in Washington. In Congress, Rayburn was still an effective Mr. Democrat; but in the Senate, the Republicans possessed a powerful Mr. Republican—Senator Robert Taft of Ohio. With Taft's leadership, the Republicans were making an effective case against the Fair Deal of Harry Truman's administration. And, with 1946 an election year for Congress, the Republicans knew that Truman's popularity had slipped fast. They moved quickly to the attack.

By summer, both Rayburn and President Truman were so concerned about the coming election they decided to campaign in Truman's home state of Missouri. Mr. Sam did not have an opponent in the Democratic primary election; so he was able to devote his full time to trying to save the Congress for the Democrats. As November came, Republican candidates were pressing hard in many Congressional districts that had been held by the Democrats. When the results came in, enough Republicans had won to give them a majority in Congress.

Sam Rayburn had won an 18th consecutive term in the House; but with the Republicans in control, he was still destined to be a loser. The gavel that had been his since 1940 would be passed on to a new Speaker. The man from Fannin County would once again take his seat on the floor of the House. Even more, Rayburn's salary dropped from $20,000 to $12,500 a year; he would no longer be provided with a Cadillac limousine and chauffeur and his large office in the House Office Building. So, at 64, he briefly considered retiring.

On the night of the election, Rayburn announced that he would not serve as the minority leader for the Democrats in the House. He decided to serve his term in Congress as the representative of the Fourth, but insisted he would become plain Congressman Rayburn once again. Immediately, the other Democrats in Washington appealed to Rayburn to change his mind—and even hinted they would draft him into the party leadership. President Truman was prepared to offer Mr. Democrat a cabinet post if he decided not to accept the minority leadership. Finally, Representative John McCormack of Massachusetts told Rayburn he was going to nominate him for minority leader in the Democrats' official meeting in Washington. When this caucus was held, Democrats from all sections of the United States rallied to the "Draft Rayburn" drive. Liberal

[132]

Democrats from the industrial metropolises of the North, conservative Democrats from the Deep South, all wanted this man who was a Democrat—as Rayburn put it—without prefix or suffix or apology. Unanimously, the caucus voted for the former Speaker to lead their minority group in the 80th Congress. And Rayburn could not find it in his heart to turn down his friends. He accepted the minority leadership, saying, "I didn't want the job and I had said I wouldn't take it. When I was voted for unanimously I yielded like I figured a good soldier should do."

When the 80th Congress opened, it elected Republican Joe Martin of Massachusetts as its new Speaker. And—if a Republican had to have the job—Rayburn could not have been happier. Joe Martin and Sam Rayburn were close friends even

Mr. Sam explained to reporters his change of heart about accepting the majority leadership.

[133]

though they were in different political parties. Mr. Sam remarked on several occasions that if he had been from Martin's state, he would have voted for him. He predicted "that history will record him as one of the great presiding officers."

At once, Martin replied: "It is a great honor to follow the honorable, able and distinguished gentleman from Texas."

Congress soon got down to business, and the two parties began their usual battles over proposed legislation. One of the greatest fights of the 80th Congress was over a measure known as the Taft-Hartley Bill to control the activities of labor unions. It was sponsored in the Senate by Mr. Republican, Senator Robert Taft. And it was opposed in the House by Mr. Democrat, Sam Rayburn. The bill was too harsh in Rayburn's opinion, being designed to punish many labor groups for striking,

Incoming Speaker Martin was congratulated by outgoing Speaker Rayburn.

[134]

even to the point of not allowing unlawful strikers to get their old jobs back. Rayburn was convinced the bill favored management over labor, and he had earlier proved that he favored neither group.

The Republicans, however, stood together firmly in the House and in the Senate, and the bill was passed and sent to President Truman for signature. When he vetoed it, the Republican Congress pushed it through into law without his signature—getting the necessary two-thirds majority of the members of both the Senate and the House of Representatives.

While Rayburn's opposition to the Taft-Hartley Act was a matter of his supporting the idea of justice, the next major legislation in the 80th Congress placed Mr. Sam in the most awkward position of his career in Congress. It was Harry Truman's civil rights program. Although not from the Old South, Rayburn lived in a section of Texas that had practiced segregation of the Negro for many years. And Sam Rayburn knew the people of the South—and his own Fourth District of Texas— were not ready to accept a sweeping change in their segregation laws. Too, the idea of direct interference in their lives from Washington was certain to meet with severe objection.

At the same time, Sam Rayburn had long supported legislation to improve life and opportunity for Negroes in his own area and throughout the United States. He had commented many times that it was saddening to see how many Negroes lived in poverty and without an opportunity to improve their standards of living. But to force integration in 1948, Rayburn knew, would create violent reaction in the South that could even destroy the entire civil rights program. He was criticized by many who wanted to push the program through the 80th Congress. But he was convinced that the time was not right for the program to succeed. Later, his decision proved to be the wise one, as he plunged headlong into the fight for true equality for all races in the United States.

In the summer of 1948, Rayburn's opponents in the Democratic primary tried to arouse the voters of the Fourth on the civil rights question. They claimed that Rayburn was trying to destroy their way of life. But at 66 years of age, Mr. Sam was no longer troubled by insults that were hurled at him in elections. Unworried, he went to the Democratic national convention in Philadelphia to serve as its permanent chairman. In his speech to the convention delegates, Mr. Democrat slammed hard at the Republican candidates, Thomas E. Dewey and Earl Warren. He pointed out that the Democrats could defend their action in *eight* Congresses while Joe Martin apologized for the *one* 80th Congress of the Republicans. In a final burst, Rayburn began asking questions, such as "Who pulled the nation out of the depression? . . . Who had helped the farmers of the country regain their lost prosperity?" With each question, Mr. Democrat gave the answer himself: "The Democrats." Soon the entire convention was caught up in the spirit of excitement and chanted their favorite answer along with him. It was a moment of unity Sam Rayburn devised to start the national convention off on the right foot. He ended his speech with a dramatic reminder of "our Democratic tradition of the 'American dream' which has been featured in the people's hearts and minds by Thomas Jefferson and Andrew Jackson, by Woodrow Wilson and by Franklin Roosevelt—and by Harry Truman."

The convention overrode protests from the South and nominated Harry Truman for President. Then, in an effort to please the Southern states who were still angry over the civil rights program, Senator Alben Barkley of Kentucky was nominated as vice president. Barkley was popular in the South, but this fact was not enough to prevent some of the Southern states from splitting away from the party in a new organization called the Dixiecrats. They nominated J. Strom Thurmond of South Carolina for President. Meanwhile, an ultraliberal group, the Progressive Party, nominated former Vice President Wallace.

But the real race, as expected, was between Republican Dewey and Democrat Truman. As the campaign started, Dewey was the overwhelming favorite, and many persons felt he was virtually in the White House as late as election night when the votes began coming in. But Truman had campaigned hard throughout the nation with his famous "give 'em hell" tactics. On Monday, September 27, 1948, the President's campaign train had even pulled into Rayburn's home town of Bonham!

Truman's train arrived at 8 P.M. and was greeted by almost 30,000 persons, who packed the streets of the small north Texas town—all the way from the train station to the football stadium. At the stadium, Mr. Sam spoke briefly to his friends of Fannin County and the Fourth District. He described the President of the United States as a "dear, personal friend of mine who has wanted to come to Bonham for a long time."

Later, Mr. Sam took the President and his family out to the family home west of town. Slowly a line began to form outside—Mr. Sam's friends who wanted to shake the hand of the President. The Secret Service objected when they saw the line increase to literally thousands. They told Rayburn it would have to be stopped, that there was too much danger. Rayburn disagreed and told the Secret Service men to stand by his side while he called each of the visitors by name, to prove they were safe. "These," Sam Rayburn said, "are my friends." As the people continued to flow through his home, Rayburn met them and greeted each by name. And the Secret Service could only stand by in quiet amazement.

Chapter 16

Back on The Rostrum

The fall of 1948 was among the happiest times in Sam Rayburn's life. He knew the national campaign was going far better for the Democrats than the "experts" thought it was. Too, his younger friend Congressman Lyndon Johnson had successfully won a close victory in the race for U. S. Senator. This was an especially happy event, for Johnson's opponent in the race had been former Governor Coke Stevenson, the man who had been effective in helping prevent Rayburn's nomination as vice president in 1944. Rayburn had worked hard to help the young congressman from the hill country north of San Antonio. With the victory over Coke Stevenson that ended his political life, Lyndon Johnson's rise began.

On November 2, the people of the United States made their surprising decision. In one of the most shocking upsets in history, the people ignored the favorite, Thomas Dewey, and reelected Harry S. Truman. The Democratic party was also swept once more into control of both houses of the Congress. For Mr. Sam, it meant the powerful gavel of the Speaker would once again be his in the 81st Congress.

With his election as Speaker on January 3, 1949, Rayburn spoke affectionately of his friends in the House who were Republicans: "One of the beautiful things about service in the House is that personal relationships and personal friendships are not divided by the center aisle. Some of the nearest and dearest friends I have ever had in the House of Representatives were on the left of the Speaker's stand. I hope it may always be so."

In the spring, still another honor came to Mr. Democrat. Along with Republican Senator Arthur Vandenberg of Michigan, Rayburn received the *Collier's* magazine award for distinguished service. Rayburn's award was given him for his

Incoming Speaker Rayburn received congratulations from outgoing Speaker Martin.

service as minority leader, when he could have taken the easier role of retiring to be simply Congressman Rayburn. He had responded to his party's need and led it vigorously during the two years he was not in the Speaker's chair. The awards included $10,000 to both Vandenberg and Rayburn, and the man from Fannin County decided immediately to use the money to fulfill an old dream he had never forgotten.

"I'm going to set up a Sam Rayburn library fund for Fannin County," the Speaker announced, "and as the years go on, I'm going to add to it as I am able. I'll build a library building to house my books, papers, and documents for future generations. The building will also have space for Bonham and Fannin County to have a library." It was an expression of appreciation Sam Rayburn felt for his neighbors. "I want to do something for the citizens of Bonham and Fannin County who have been so fine to me all these years." The slow process began with the $10,000 award that started what would later become one of Bonham's most beloved landmarks.

But honors such as the *Collier's* award come from hard work, and Mr. Sam turned his attention to the legislative program of the new 81st Congress. One of the first important items was a revision of the Taft-Hartley Act, which had been passed by the Republican-controlled 80th Congress. Immediately, the Speaker went to work. He had several conferences with President Truman to find an effective way to handle the situation. Rayburn realized that the Taft-Hartley Act was too strong in its punishment of labor unions. At the same time, he felt it was not entirely a bad law, and he decided to seek a compromise that would keep its best features. Rayburn's solution was a plan that would retain Taft-Hartley's provision allowing the President to prevent strikes that interfere with the national welfare. Rayburn also proposed to have a joint Congressional

Committee, composed of members of the Senate and the House, to study labor relations. The committee would have an opportunity to find a solution to labor-management arguments before action by the President would become necessary.

The Speaker's plan, of course, was not popular with labor union leaders such as John L. Lewis of the United Mine Workers. And once again, members of the Congress found it difficult to figure out the man from Fannin County. He continued his established policy of not being "pro-labor" or "pro-management." In keeping the Presidential authority to prevent strikes, labor felt Rayburn was deserting their cause. This was not the case. Rayburn was simply seeking a fair way to deal with a difficult problem. And his attitude was typical; if some did not like his opinion, he could not have cared less.

Meanwhile, still another controversy was shaping up in Washington involving the ownership of the tidelands areas surrounding the coastlines of the United States. The states claimed that they owned the area, but the Supreme Court had ruled against them. Texas, in particular, wanted to retain the oil rights to its 10-mile zone of tidelands areas extending into the Gulf of Mexico. It was expected that the tidelands areas would produce millions of dollars worth of oil, and Texas wanted the revenue from this production rather than have the money go into the federal treasury.

Mr. Sam's compromise bill gave to Texas 62½ percent of the oil and mineral rights inside the ten-mile tidelands area. Beyond the ten-mile limit, Texas was to receive one-half of all oil and mineral rights in an area extending about 140 miles into the Gulf of Mexico. Because of the presence of large salt domes which probably held oil in the outer area, Rayburn believed his compromise would enable Texas to keep most of the profit from the tidelands and still profit from the federal area beyond.

[141]

But, just as with his position on civil rights and the Taft-Hartley Act, many people disagreed with the man from Fannin. It was an absolute impossibility to please all of the people. Sam Rayburn did not try. Instead, he took steps in the direction of finding solutions that would work—and that would be fair to all of the parties involved in the disputes.

Toward the end of 1949, the political battles in Washington were suspended for a few weeks, and the Speaker took a trip to Houston for a huge gathering of Democrats from all over the states. The star of the show was Mr. Democrat himself, Speaker Sam Rayburn. It was a rare moment in which the liberal and conservative wings of the Democratic Party in Texas came together briefly. Altogether, it was a pleasing trip.

But Rayburn's trips into the large cities in Texas were usually confusing. In Dallas and in Houston, the ultraconservatives that originally were part of W. Lee O'Daniel's Texas Regulars were becoming more and more powerful. Even though Lyndon Johnson had blasted Coke Stevenson into political obscurity, Stevenson had been quickly replaced. Even some of the metropolitan newspapers took a rather unusual position. They urged all persons to vote in the Democratic primary elections, and then often urged these same voters to support Republican candidates in the general elections in the fall. To Rayburn, this was ridiculous. Voting to select a candidate for the Democratic party seemed to mean a person was a Democrat. To change completely in a matter of weeks and vote for a Republican in the general election did not strike Rayburn as an honest way to vote.

As time went on, many of the Texas Regulars became "Shivercrats" in support of ultraconservative Governor Allan Shivers. Later many of these same people began to drift slowly into the Republican Party—where they perhaps should have been in the first place, according to Mr. Sam. Rayburn had been a Democrat throughout his political life and he had never forgotten Cactus Jack Garner's advice: "Sam, stay hitched!" Rayburn often admitted that he would have voted for Republican Joe Martin if we were from Martin's district in Massachusetts, and he was quick to point out that many of the greatest and most patriotic Americans were in the Republican party. But to Rayburn, they should *stay* in the Republican party if that was their preference, instead of switching back and forth.

The next few months brought even more honors to the most famous Democrat in the nation. He was elected in November of 1949 to honorary membership in the Phi Beta Kappa chapter at the University of Texas. In May of 1950, Rayburn was awarded an honorary Doctor of Humanities degree by Austin College in Sherman, one of the principal towns in his Fourth District. In the next month, National University made the Speaker an honorary Doctor of Laws. And the following month, July, the Democrats of the Fourth gave him still another tribute by electing him without opposition to his 20th consecutive term in the House of Representatives. As the honors followed one another, the Speaker watched with increasing concern the "police action" in far away Korea that had begun in late June of 1950. President Truman called on him to help defend the administration position of fighting the Communists in South Korea.

By November of 1950, the United Nations forces, comprised mostly of United States troops under the command of General Douglas MacArthur, had pushed the invading North Koreans back to their own area behind the 38th parallel. As the 82nd Congress opened for its first session early in 1951, the Korean situation was under control, even though the fighting was still going on. In a quiet voting that surprised not a single member, the House of Representatives named Sam Rayburn of Texas as its Speaker. It was the sixth time Rayburn had received the honor, and he was closing in fast on even more Congressional records.

On January 30, 1951, when the stocky, bald man from Fannin County took his seat in the great chair on the House rostrum, he pushed ahead in length of service, passing one of the great Americans and great Speakers in history, Henry Clay, who had served 3,056½ days as Speaker of the House. But now the gavel had been held by Sam Rayburn for one day longer. "Sam Rayburn Day" followed in the House on January 31, with Democrats and Republicans uniting in tributes.

As spring came there was growing tension between the President of the United States and his commander in Korea. General MacArthur wanted to pursue the Chinese Communist army beyond the 38th parallel, while President Truman felt that it would be enough to drive the Communist forces out of South Korea. It made no sense to MacArthur for an army to fight without a chance at a clear victory—and he said so on several occasions. Finally, President Truman requested that McArthur clear his policy statements through the Defense Department. When MacArthur refused, the President relieved MacArthur of his command. On his return to the United States, thousands greeted him as a national hero, while many others agreed with the President. Among them was Speaker Sam Rayburn. To him it was a case of the authority of the Presidency— and the civilian government—over military leaders. It had nothing to do with Rayburn's respect for MacArthur as a great general and even as a great American.

Through the remainder of 1951, Rayburn defended the Truman administration's policies in Korea as well as at home. The Speaker pointed out that action in blocking the Communist take-over in Korea had "put a chill into the men of the Kremlin and had fired with renewed faith the hearts of free men the world over." On the civil rights question, the man from Fannin County warned the Southern states that they would have to give their Negro citizens a better break if they wanted to prevent federal action. And to the Dixiecrats he issued a stern warning: if they allowed the Republicans to gain control of the Congress, they would be passed over when the committee assignments were made. In simple language, he reminded the Dixiecrat politicians they had better get back into the Democratic fold before the 1952 elections wiped them out. Sam Rayburn did not hesitate to tell anyone what he thought—especially Democrats who failed to "stay hitched."

The second session of the 82nd Congress opened a little later than usual in January of 1952, and the Speaker was thus able to celebrate his 70th birthday at home in Bonham. It was a happy time in the big white house, with several of Mr. Sam's brothers and sisters there for the Sunday birthday dinner. Among them, of course, was Rayburn's favorite, his sister Lucinda. Miss Lou had even been Rayburn's official hostess in Washington from time to time, a natural development of Mr. Sam's deep affection for her. The birthday party was a huge success and served as a happy beginning for his 71st year.

It was hard for many people to believe Mr. Sam had reached this age, for his appearance had hardly changed at all. His baldness had come early in his life and was not, therefore, a mark of age. Rayburn was still as active and as energetic as ever, enjoying his work on the ranch as well as in Congress. This great vitality seemed to amaze many people. Press photographers often came to Bonham when the Speaker was there to take pictures of him working with his cattle or swinging a heavy axe to chop some wood for the bunkhouse stove.

Blowing out the candles at a Washington birthday party given by Lyndon Johnson

Rayburn returned to Washington for the opening of Congress on January 8, eager to see what the months ahead would bring. It was an election year both for the Congress and the White House. No one knew if Harry Truman would seek another term in office; so the prospects of a wide open Democratic convention were good. Afterward would come the campaign, and finally the election itself. To Mr. Sam, it was a familiar pattern, which he always enjoyed. But the problems that came up in the spring caught the Speaker's full attention. It was a matter, once again, of agriculture. Two amendments had been brought forward on the floor of the House that would cut $75,-000,000 from the soil conservation bill.

Immediately, the man from Fannin swung into action. The word went out that Rayburn was going to fight the amendments personally from the floor. He had been a frequent and effective speechmaker in the days before he was elected Speaker. And when he served as minority leader of the 80th Congress, he often made speeches from the floor. But as Speaker of the House, Rayburn used his influence, leadership, and gavel to push through his favored bills. This legislation was something special, however, and Rayburn decided to give it the full treatment. When the word was out that "Mr. Sam is up!" the Congress of the United States always took on a slightly different atmosphere. The galleries quickly filled with visitors and reporters, and Congressmen who might otherwise have been elsewhere made it a point to be in their appointed seats.

In a thorough examination of soil conservation, Rayburn pointed out to the Congressmen from large cities· that their constituents would be walking the streets in hunger if the farmers of the nation were not given a way to rebuild the soil. When he was finished, Rayburn remained on the floor of the House as the voting began. Carefully, he watched until it was clear that the fight had been won by a large majority, with much of his help coming from his Republican friends.

Before the spring was over, Harry Truman announced his decision: he would not seek the Presidential nomination in the convention that summer. Immediately, likely candidates began to be discussed: Fred Vinson, Adlai Stevenson, Vice President Alben Barkley—and, once again—Sam Rayburn. But again it was the same story among the Democrats in Texas. It would be difficult to get the ultraconservatives of the party to support the Speaker. This group, under the leadership of Governor Allan Shivers, would have been considered ultraconservative even if they had been in the Republican Party. That they somehow felt they were Democrats at all merely points up the confusion of politics in Rayburn's home state.

Miss Lou and Mr. Sam

[148]

Still the talk of Sam Rayburn for President continued. One of his strongest supporters was Senator Mike Monroney of Oklahoma, who believed that the convention would not be able to nominate a candidate on an early ballot. With a deadlock, the delegates would then be ready to switch to a new candidate, such as Rayburn.

For his own part, Mr. Sam expressed only mild interest in the Presidential nomination. He stated bluntly that he was not going to be an active candidate. His only concession to the many Democrats who were urging him to run was to state that if the convention turned to him after a deadlock, he would accept the nomination. But he made it obvious that he was not seeking the nomination in any way. At the convention, he planned to concentrate on his job of serving as permanent chairman, a big enough assignment to occupy all his time. He even ignored the fact that a man named Reagan Brown was campaigning against him for his seat in the House.

The man from Fannin County banged the new Democratic Convention to order in late July of 1952, but one thing was different from previous conventions. He had served as a delegate and as permanent chairman in 1948, but this year, he also became a television star. The major networks telecast the entire convention, and it was Sam Rayburn's sternness and sparkling laughter the voters of the country saw most. He handled the wild convention as if it were his personal property, banging the gavel to clear the aisles and scowling at the delegates who would not obey. Almost fearsome at times, the Rayburn image on the television screen was often relieved by his flashes of wit and humor in handling the thousands of people on the convention floor and in the galleries.

Mr. Sam became a national personality.

Chapter 17

Down—and Up Again

O n the third ballot, Adlai E. Stevenson became the 1952 Democratic nominee for the Presidency. After his nomination, a meeting was held late at night between President Truman, Speaker Rayburn, and the nominee. Several men had been discussed for the vice presidential nomination when Mr. Sam turned to Stevenson and asked him for his preference. The result was the nomination of John Sparkman of Alabama for vice president in an effort to hold the South in line.

Meanwhile, the Republican Party made its own nomination of General Dwight D. Eisenhower and Richard M. Nixon. A few years earlier, Eisenhower had been approached by both political parties as a possible candidate in the 1948 campaign. At the time he did not have a clear preference in political parties, and his decision was to not run on either ticket. He had served instead as the president of Columbia University and slowly came to the decision that he was more a Republican than a Democrat. It was a decision that spelled political doom for Mr.

Republican—Senator Robert A. Taft—who was trying desperately to gain his party's nomination.

As Mr. Republican, Senator Taft represented the "Old Guard" of his party, its most conservative members. Eisenhower, on the other hand, was more liberal, and was not able to decide quickly that he was not really a Democrat. He was not a professional politician, but he was tremendously popular with the people. His broad and happy smile beamed with honest enthusiasm. The slogan "I like Ike" caught on immediately.

Eisenhower had been born in Sam Rayburn's Fourth District of Texas, in the town of Denison near the Red River. And it was in Texas that one of the sharpest battles developed in the 1948 campaign. Naturally enough, Mr. Sam was in the thick of it, as the fight centered on the basic split in the state Democratic party. For years it had been a thorn in the Speaker's side. In 1952 it became a spear!.

Under the leadership of Governor Allan Shivers, the "Democrats for Eisenhower" movement was formed. As the head of the party in Texas, Shivers devised a way for Democrats there to vote for Eisenhower and still remain Democrats! He suggested that Eisenhower's name appear on the ballot under the Democratic column as well as the Republican. Shivers himself even took an active part in the campaign to defeat Stevenson in Texas. He reminded the voters of the tidelands issue of the previous Congress and claimed that under Eisenhower this money would remain in the state. Billboards with Eisenhower wearing a typical Texas-style hat were put up on most of the highways of the state, reminding the people of Eisenhower's brief residence in Denison when he was a baby.

Such Democrats as Rayburn and Lyndon Johnson fought hard to save Texas for Stevenson; but it was the same story as in many states: Ike's tremendous popularity was too much to

[151]

overcome. Adlai Stevenson was a polished and effective speaker, but he did not have the magical appeal of the famous general. When November came, the Republican Party gained the Presidency for the first time since Herbert Hoover's election in 1928, rolling up 442 electoral votes to Stevenson's 89.

As the election returns came in, Rayburn once more saw the Democratic majority in Congress slip away—and with it his own job as the Speaker of the House. Again, he would have to decide between being merely Congressman Rayburn or the minority leader. But this time, the decision was easier, and the man from Fannin County was ready to lead the Democrats of the House from the floor.

Six years earlier, Sam Rayburn had escorted his Massachusetts friend Joe Martin to the rostrum in a spirit of good humor. In the opening session of the 83rd Congress early in January of 1953, he did it again. Only three days before his 71st birthday, Mr. Sam lost his cherished position in the House. "Today," he said to his fellow Congressman with the famous twinkle in his usually serious eyes, "I come back to present that same great American to be Speaker of the House—again temporarily!"

As the Eisenhower administration began, Mr. Sam reached a new plateau in his career in Congress. With his own protégé Lyndon Johnson a powerful man in the Senate, Rayburn was by far the most influential man on Capitol Hill, even though his own party was not in power. Early in February, 1953, this was demonstrated when Congress selected Democrat Rayburn to escort the new Republican President to the rostrum for his State of the Union message. At first, Eisenhower was slow to realize how important Rayburn's friendship could be; but later he was forced to depend on the man from Fannin County to get much of his legislation passed by the House.

From the floor of the House, the Republican leadership felt the sting of Rayburn's anger early in the 83rd Congress. For days the Republicans had been making speeches about their great November victory. But some members were managing to insult the Democrats more than they were praising the Republicans. At last, Mr. Sam had had enough—and he let the Congress know it. "I know how to cause trouble if I want to, for I know something about the rules of the House and the rights of the minority," he warned darkly. He also reminded the Congress that the victory in November was an Eisenhower victory more than it was a Republican one, and that 1954 could change things entirely. If some of the Republican members wanted to play that way, it was all right with Mr. Sam. But they should be prepared to take some of the same treatment.

When an Eisenhower health insurance bill was being debated, Rayburn showed them what he meant. Such a bill did not have much support from the conservative wing of the Republican Party; the bill needed minority Democrat votes to put it through. Rayburn thought it was a good bill and had said so. But at the time he thought it was more important to show the Republicans they could not ride over the Democrats in the House. During his own years as Speaker, he had always treated the Republicans fairly—and had received valuable support from such Republican leaders as Joe Martin. Rayburn knew he needed the Republicans to get many of his own bills passed. Now, he would demonstrate that the Republicans needed him as well. In a surprising move, the minority leader withheld the support of the Democrats. Also lacking was the conservative Republican strength—and the bill fell dead in the House. It was a lesson well taught by the master of both passing *and* defeating legislation!

[153]

During the remaining months of the first session of the 83rd Congress, the minority leader fought for such measures as soil conservation, free trade with other nations, and the important Mutual Security Act. In debate, Rayburn argued against cutting Eisenhower's budget. Some of the conservatives wanted to trim it by $2,500,000,000, and Rayburn was convinced that such a cut would endanger the safety of the free world from Communism. Speaker Joe Martin left the rostrum to make a speech in full agreement with Rayburn and Eisenhower. Among them, their influence was sufficient to get the bill passed by the House.

With the end of the first session, Rayburn headed for home. During a short vacation, he worked with his cattle in Texas' scorching August sun. Then, he turned his attention to mending the badly torn fences of the Democratic party in his home state. Since Texas had voted for Eisenhower, Rayburn urged in a speech in San Antonio that these people who had so voted should vote in the Republican primary next time. The Republicans were now building a strong organization in the state's largest city, Houston, and in Dallas. San Antonio, however, remained a Democratic stronghold among Texas' three largest cities.

Mr. Sam returned to Washington for the second session of the 83rd Congress, which opened on his 72nd birthday, January 6, 1954. The year got off to a good start for Rayburn, with a birthday message from the President. After a full year of experience, Eisenhower was beginning to realize how much help Democrats like Rayburn could be. Although they were in different parties, the two men were reasonably close in their view of what the federal government should do. For this reason, Eisenhower was just as unhappy as Rayburn when Republican Senator McCarthy of Wisconsin began his campaign of slander.

[154]

Unfortunately, the leadership of the Republican Party was not able to get McCarthy to stop his insults. He repeatedly referred to the administrations of Presidents Roosevelt and Truman as "20 years of treason," and he insisted the Democrats had been too soft in their attitude toward Communism. In particular, McCarthy leveled vicious attacks at Truman. To these, Sam Rayburn pointed out that the Democrats would never "attack the integrity of the President of the United States, because we have too much respect for that great office and too much respect for the man that is in it."

Still, the Wisconsin Senator raved on, accusing the Democratic party in general of treason against the United States. Finally, Mr. Sam sent a message to President Eisenhower. It was, in actuality, a warning to the Republican Senator. As the man from Fannin County said on several occasions during the early months of 1954, "Some of our backs are getting mighty sore." Eisenhower responded by commenting on the poor taste of McCarthy's attack in such serious times. He expressed the hope that the insults would be cut off by Republicans.

But the damage already was done in the Congress. While Rayburn's personal relations with the President were not disturbed, the gap between the two great parties on Capitol Hill grew into a chasm. Through the remainder of the 83rd Congress, Republicans and Democrats were opposed on almost every bill that was presented. On one of these, Rayburn fought especially hard. It was a new Republican tax bill, and Mr. Sam pointed out that only six families out of every 1,000 would receive $814,000,000 in tax reduction, while most of the remaining citizens would receive very little relief from their tax burden. Mr. Democrat attacked the bill as typical Republican legislation that favored the wealthy, but the Republican majority was too much for him to overcome and the bill was passed.

As Congress neared the time for adjournment, Rayburn blasted away at its record and at the entire Eisenhower administration. In one of his first comments on the coming Congressional election in 1954, Mr. Sam described the Eisenhower administration as being about as "forward looking as yesterday"! It was a theme he used to hammer home his dissatisfaction with the Republican control of Congress. At home in the Fourth District, a man named A. G. McRae announced for Congress in the Democratic primary. Without even returning for a campaign, Mr. Sam swamped his opponent in defeat. It was Mr. Democrat's 22nd consecutive victory in the Fourth District.

With the victory at the polls in July behind him, Sam Rayburn concentrated on helping the Democrats regain control of the House and Senate in Washington. Rayburn was certain the Republican victory in 1952 had been more Eisenhower's than his party's, and that in 1954 the people would turn to the Democrats again. His prediction was correct, for in the fall election the Democrats regained control of both houses of Congress. Their advantage in the Senate was small, but it was enough to elect Lyndon B. Johnson as majority leader. And, of course, it meant the return of Sam Rayburn to the Speaker's rostrum in the House of Representatives.

When the 84th Congress of the United States opened on January 6, 1955, Sam Rayburn of Texas mounted the steps that led to the great Speaker's chair, accepting his sixth full term in the highest office in the legislative branch of the government. And, although he did not know it at the time, the great chair was his alone. Never again during his lifetime would any other man be addressed with the title of Speaker.

Chapter 18

Above Party Lines

O ne of the first important measures the 84th Congress considered was the renewal of the Reciprocal Trade Act, a law that provided lower tariffs and free trade with other nations. Rayburn, as he had been throughout his years in the House, was for the low tariff. The President, too, gave it his full support as part of the "new Republican" philosophy of "trade, not aid" to foreign nations. Still, the true conservatives who continued to want a high, protective tariff for United States industry almost beat down the Reciprocal Trade program. When it appeared that the Act might not be renewed, Speaker Rayburn left the rostrum to make a personal plea on the floor of the House.

Eisenhower waited anxiously for the result of the voting. He wanted the bill to be renewed, and he was dependent on Democrat Rayburn to get it through the Congress. When the votes were counted, the man from Fannin County had scored another victory as Congressman after Congressman switched his vote after hearing his appeal.

Sam Rayburn's own party soon gave him the formal recognition he deserved, even though President Eisenhower largely ignored the Speaker's help. On April 16, 1955, the Democratic party replaced its usual Jefferson-Jackson Day dinner with a testimonial dinner in honor of Sam Rayburn. The dinner was one of the $100-a-plate affairs that political parties use to build up their funds. For the Democratic party, the Rayburn Testimonial Dinner proved to be one of the most successful fundraisers in its history, as almost 4,000 persons attended in the National Guard Armory. Among them were Mrs. Woodrow Wilson, Mrs. Eleanor Roosevelt, former President and Mrs. Harry Truman. Such important Democrats as Adlai Stevenson and Lyndon Johnson helped pay tribute to the most famous living Democrat of them all: Sam Rayburn. High above the crowd were two pictures of the usual honorees—Thomas Jefferson and Andrew Jackson. But these earlier Democrats took second place on April 16 to a larger picture of the man from Fannin County.

The 73-year-old Speaker sat quietly as, one after another, the most important members of his "crowd" honored him with brief speeches. Some, such as the "Shivercrat" Democrats, he had argued with on occasion; others, such as Senate Majority Leader Lyndon Johnson, had always fought on his side. But all were that day his friends. As they tried to discuss the accomplishments of Rayburn's years in the Congress, they suffered the usual trouble of trying to find language to describe true greatness. At last, the time came for the Speaker himself to address the audience. When he stood up, the crowd burst into tremendous applause. On and on the ovation went, and the man from Fannin County could hardly believe it was all for him. Quietly he stood until at last their applause rose in a great wave as the band struck up "The Eyes of Texas." The people stood, and the sound of Rayburn's Texas music and their continuing ovation was at last too much. Mr. Sam's eyes filled with tears, but as the tears streamed down his face, the Speaker broke into a wide grin and waved at the thousands before him. Of all the moments in Mr. Sam's life, this more than any other was *his!*

In his own speech Rayburn discussed the past and the role of the Democratic party in it—and what it could look forward to in the future. "In the fullness of time and service to the nation, the Democratic Party has come to be more than a political party. It has become an Idea; an essential part of the American Idea. Political parties have their victories and defeats but great ideas go on forever. Hence we Democrats may look with equal serenity to 1956 or to 1976." In his closing remarks, Mr. Sam discussed the conditions of the world in 1955: "Today darkness broods over the face of the earth. Evil stalks the hills. No man knows what devouring monsters tomorrow may bring. May I say, then, to my countrymen—let us in this desperate hour nobly conceive and nobly act in the greatness that is our heritage and our light and our life. So doing, within the eye of God, we shall triumph over evil as did the founders of this great Republic."

It was a great night for Sam Rayburn; so it was also a great night for Rayburn's great Republic!

Throughout the year, even more honors came to the Speaker. On May 30, 1955, Mr. Sam addressed the graduating class at the University of West Virginia, and afterward received its Doctor of Laws degree. In the fall, "Sam Rayburn Day" was held in Fort Worth; and in Dallas there was another dinner at State Fair Park with 5,000 persons attending. But even with all this extra activity, Rayburn kept a tight hold on the House of Representatives, pushing through about 60 of the bills Eisenhower sent to Capitol Hill. He pointed out that the Democratic Congress had been far more cooperative with Eisenhower's program than the Republican-controlled 83rd had been.

In October, the first hint appeared of the coming Presidential election year as the newspapers of the nation carried a story about an important meeting in the Hill Country north of San Antonio. At Lyndon B. Johnson's ranch, a meeting was attended by Johnson, Adlai Stevenson, and Sam Rayburn. Doubtless the Democratic national convention ·in the summer of 1956 was one of the major topics discussed. With the beginning of the new year, the battle lines for the Democratic Presidential nomination were being drawn, and Sam Rayburn announced that his own choice was Lyndon B. Johnson. Rayburn knew his announcement would not come as a surprise— and that it would probably cause a showdown fight with Governor Allan Shivers for control of the Texas delegation.

But as the year drew to an end, Sam Rayburn's thoughts pulled temporarily away from politics. The fund for his library project in Bonham had grown from the original $10,000 to $450,000. In a typical Rayburn attitude, the Speaker insisted that each person's donation would be kept secret, indicating his appreciation for the smallest gifts as well as the large ones that ran into thousands of dollars. The groundbreaking ceremonies for the library were held in December on a spacious lot between Sam Rayburn's home and downtown Bonham. As the work began, Rayburn's dream was at last coming to life.

Early in 1956, the expected battle between Rayburn and Governor Shivers for control of the Texas delegation started. The fight centered on Rayburn's backing of Lyndon Johnson as Texas' "favorite son" candidate for the Democratic Presidential nomination. On a national television program, "Meet the Press," Shivers stated that he would like to know exactly what Johnson's views were, even though he had always admired the Senator. Johnson replied later by pointing out that he had never been a member of any political group other than the Democratic party. "Nor," he said, "have I been the errand boy of the reactionary big business or the Republican Party."

Sam Rayburn appealed to the Democrats of the state to elect delegates who would support a truly Democratic leadership. The response was not denied. Allan Shivers had been considered unbeatable in a political battle. But that was before he met Sam Rayburn in a fight for the people's vote. The Texas delegation went to Sam Rayburn and Lyndon Johnson.

At the convention in June, 1956, Speaker Rayburn was elected permanent chairman for the third time. Once more the

The demonstration for Mr. Democrat as he took up the gavel as permanent chairman of the 1956 Democratic convention

[161]

famous bald head of the man from Fannin County was seen on television screens in millions of homes. The Rayburn sternness this time, however, was tempered with sadness; for only a few months earlier his beloved sister Lucinda had died of cancer. But even with the lingering memory of her death on his mind, Sam Rayburn used his technique in handling political conventions more masterfully than ever before. One of Mr. Sam's parliamentary tricks in 1956 was to follow this pattern for taking a vote on an issue that was sure to win. "Those in favor say aye." A pause. "There are no noes." Another pause, and then a hard crack of the nation's most famous gavel. "It is unanimous!"

The result was that Rayburn was by far the most interesting person in both political conventions, as the two parties duplicated their choice of four years earlier by naming Eisenhower and Stevenson as their Presidential nominees. Sadly, Mr. Democrat saw the campaign during the fall go in much the same way as it had in 1952. It was hardly a shock when 35,-000,000 votes went to Eisenhower and only 26,000,000 to Stevenson. In the electoral college, the vote was 457 votes to 74.

It was not, however, a total defeat for Mr. Sam's "crowd." For the people voted to keep the Democratic majorities in both the House of Representatives and in the Senate. In the Fourth District, Rayburn was not opposed. Rayburn was elected, on January 3, 1957, to a seventh full term as the Speaker of the House; and in the Senate, his protégé Lyndon Johnson scored a close victory to be elected majority leader.

Mr. Sam's birthday came only a few days after the opening of the 85th Congress. At 75, the great Speaker remarked that he felt like a two-year-old colt and that he wanted "to see a lot of years to come." The hard pace at which the Speaker worked during the 85th Congress proved that he meant what he said. It appeared that the man in the Speaker's chair was as indestructible as Congress itself. Even his appearance had not changed much as the years continued to roll by; his weight remained exactly the same as it had been when he first entered Congress in 1913, 44 years before. He stood with the same square set to his shoulders, and his eyes—if somewhat weaker —still bristled and sparkled with wisdom and warm humor.

His weekly press conferences in his office were still among the most popular with Washington reporters, for Rayburn was also famed for his friendly attitude and straight answers to the press. The sessions were always informal. The Speaker would lean back in the big leather chair behind his desk, light a cigarette, and casually discuss the major questions of the times. Always with a view to the future, Rayburn remained progressive in his attitude on all subjects and used his 50 years of total legislative service in the wisest possible way. The past was the background, the framework to use in judging the present and in planning for the future.

In June of 1957, the power of the Speaker received one of its rare tests. Earlier—in 1952 and in 1955—Rayburn had declared that televising House committee meetings would not be allowed. There was a rule that House proceedings could not be broadcast, and Rayburn felt it was also applicable to any meeting of a House committee. The entire issue flared up once more in 1957 when the House Committee on Un-American Activities permitted the televising of its meetings. In particular, Rayburn objected to the filming of a meeting of the committee in San Francisco. But a spokesman of the committee announced that since the meetings were not in Washington, the rule did not apply. The committee was meeting in federal courtrooms, said the spokesman, and its action was guided by the policy of the federal court it was using.

[163]

This, of course, did not make any sense at all to Sam Rayburn, and he said so rather pointedly. He ordered the committee to discontinue televising and filming its meetings. Francis E. Walter of Pennsylvania, the chairman of the committee, bluntly replied: "There is no such rule."

When Walter's message reached Rayburn's office in the Capitol, Mr. Sam read it slowly. "No comment," was his only reply. The final answer to Representative Walter came from the House of Representatives itself, which backed Sam Rayburn's ruling almost unanimously. It marked not only the end of televised House committee meetings, but also a sharp decline in the influence of Congressman Walter during the next several months.

THE SAM RAYBURN LIBRARY

Mr. Sam at his desk in his office in the
Sam Rayburn Library

A more pleasant event for Mr. Sam took place in the fall of the year when his library was formally opened on October 9, 1957. Again, the little town of Bonham was a gathering place for some of the nation's most important lawmakers. In addition to Harry Truman and Lyndon Johnson, even Secretary of Treasury Robert Anderson of Eisenhower's administration came.

Constructed of white Georgian marble, the Sam Rayburn Library was built at a cost of $452,000. A graceful, U-shaped driveway leads to the library, which is located at the top of a gentle hill four blocks from the downtown area. The heavy glass doors have the carved initials S R on them, a reminder of Mr. Sam's habit of initialing on page 99 each book he finished. Book after book may be taken from the shelves of the library—and most of them bear the mark that indicated they have been read by Mr. Sam.

Just inside the door is a bronze plaque that reads:

Erected 1956 by
THE SAM RAYBURN FOUNDATION
To preserve to posterity the official records of the
Honorable Sam Rayburn, member of Congress from
the Fourth Congressional District, Speaker of the
House of Representatives for a longer period than
any other man in the history of the nation.
1940—1947
1949—1953   1955—1961

Inside is the Speaker's personal library, the published records of the Congress of the United States from the first Continental Congress of 1774 to the present time, books of American history, biographies and writings of Presidents of the

United States and other important Americans. In the basements are the files of Sam Rayburn's correspondence with the people of the Fourth District and personal records of his many years in the Congress. The walls throughout the library are lined with photographs that record his association with the history of his country since Woodrow Wilson. But the most interesting of all the rooms in the library is Mr. Sam's office itself. It is an exact duplicate of his office in Washington, even to the flooring and the high vaulted ceiling. His furniture—the big red leather chairs and his huge desk—have been moved to Bonham. Mr. Sam himself took new furnishings for his Capitol office.

With the completion of the library in Bonham, Mr. Sam turned to architecture in other areas—this time in Washington, D. C. He began formulating a plan to have the east front of the Capitol remodeled! Earlier efforts to improve the crumbling east front had failed; but by the start of 1958, Rayburn decided to give the project the full force of his personal attention. He pointed out that engineers claimed the east front was actually a hazard and that in remodeling it, nothing of beauty would be destroyed. "Those beautiful pieces of cornice up there are falling off. They can't be replaced. . . ." Going further, Rayburn explained that the remodeling would provide as many as 54 additional offices in the Capitol Building. By springtime of 1958, Rayburn made a plea for the project at the National Press Club in Washington. "It boils down to this," Mr. Sam said bluntly. "The stones we can't save. The design we can. And we can save it better and more safely on a new wall 32½ feet to the east!" As usual, Mr. Sam got his way with the Congress of the United States.

That summer Rayburn was unopposed for Congressman in the Fourth District, and there was no really good reason for him to leave the Speaker's chair for a trip home. But at 76, no one in the House questioned the decisions of the Congress' most distinguished member. Quietly, he decided to make a quick trip home.

The occasion was a homecoming celebration in the tiny Fannin County community of Flag Springs. The former students gathered at the one-room school house. Many of them had known Sam in schoolboy days. They were thinking and talking about their most honored fellow student when—amazingly enough—in walked Sam Rayburn himself! Unannounced, the man from Fannin County returned to help celebrate with his friends their happiest of all homecomings! "I love this ground," the Speaker said; "it is my native heath."

In this simple action lies much of the greatness of the man. Sam Rayburn was always happy to have the background that was his. He would not have traded his school days in Flag Springs and later at Mayo College for an education at Yale or Harvard. He was content to be what he was. His famous remark, "You know, I just missed being a tenant farmer by a gnat's heel," describes his attitude. He was always close to the people of his home, his "native heath"; he was always one of them, whether in Bonham or in the highest office in the House. He never forgot the small—often tiny—difference between success and failure. And he loved the simple rolling countryside of the Fourth District, not for its great mountains or its marvelous seacoast or its wonderful climate—for it has none of these. He loved it for the best reason of all: it was *his*, the country of his childhood, his youth, his manhood, and his life itself.

The election of the fall brought a continuing happiness to the great man from Fannin County. His "crowd," the Democrats, swept to another victory in the Congressional races around the nation. It was the most one sided victory the Democratic party had enjoyed since the great one of 1936. In the House, Democrats outnumbered Republicans by 282 to 153. And in the Senate, they held 62 seats while the Republicans kept only 34. Sam Rayburn could not have been happier.

But early in 1959, much of his joy over the Democratic victory was snatched away in a bitter disappointment. Surprisingly enough, it came from the Republicans! The G.O.P. was having a rather violent reaction to their heavy Congressional losses in the recent election. President Eisenhower himself was thoroughly unhappy with the Republican's showing. And, when talk began of reorganizing the leadership in the House of Representatives, Eisenhower apparently decided this was not a particularly bad idea. One of Eisenhower's principal advisers, Sherman Adams, also favored some changes in the Republican organization on Capitol Hill.

The chief target for the change turned out to be Sam Rayburn's good friend Joe Martin of Massachusetts, the man who had served so well as Speaker during the terms when Rayburn was forced to operate from the floor of the House. A great leader of the Republicans, Martin had distinguished himself as a vigorous spokesman when his party was in the minority. During the Congresses that were controlled by the Republicans, he served as Speaker with the same fairness and loyalty to the House that marked Rayburn's own career. But in a sweeping change, the Republicans decided to ignore Martin as their minority leader in the 86th Congress. Instead, they elected a younger man, Representative Charles Halleck of Indiana.

When Sam Rayburn heard the news, it struck him as a terrible miscarriage of justice. In his mid-70's himself, he knew that age was not really the reason for Martin's having been passed over. Had a similar event taken place in Rayburn's own party, it would have felt the full force of the Speaker's anger, a fact that doubtless kept many of the Democrats in line over the years. Rayburn had already acquired a well filled "Boot Hill" of his own composed of those who had made the mistake of crossing him. The list included more than 20 defeated candidates in the Fourth District, and former Governors Coke Stevenson, W. Lee O'Daniel, and Allan Shivers. It also included a young Republican Congressman named Bruce Alger of Dallas, whom Rayburn kept "buried in the woodwork of the House."

But the Republicans' affairs were theirs alone—and Rayburn was wise enough not to enter them. Still, he could not fail to express his sorrow over his friend's misfortune. On the night of the Republican caucus that voted Martin out of the leadership, Rayburn was attending a party at the Women's National Democratic Club in Washington. While the Speaker was talking with a group of guests, he glanced toward the door just as Joe Martin entered the room. The Speaker excused himself and went straight to his friend. In a gesture they both understood, Mr. Sam put his arm around the former Republican Speaker.

"Do you have a cubbyhole for me anywhere?" Joe Martin asked.

Rayburn studied his friend's face, realizing the great compliment Martin was paying him by coming to a Democratic Party gathering.

"Joe," Mr. Sam drawled, "you can have anything you want!"

Moved by the great sincerity of Rayburn's friendship which had never known the absurdity of party lines, Joe Martin's eyes quickly filled with tears. It was good to have a friend like Sam Rayburn of Fannin County at a moment like this.

Chapter 19

Making a Vice President

✦

In the 86th Congress of the United States, Sam Rayburn began his eighth term as Speaker of the House on January 7, 1959. Late in February, Rayburn lifted a shovelful of dirt and work began on the east front of the Capitol Building in Washington. Happily, he predicted that the new front would be ready for the inauguration of the next President in 1961. Already the man from Fannin County was making plans for the 1960 Presidential campaign.

Rayburn was closing in fast on still another important point in his career as a lawmaker. On March 5, 1959, he broke the 46-year record of another historic and powerful Speaker, the famous Joe Cannon. A few years later, Rayburn was honored in the Supreme Court building by a group of Senators who had served with him earlier in the House of Representatives. Among them, however, was one man who was no longer a Senator—but who came anyway—Vice President Richard Nixon. Rayburn and Nixon had never been close, certainly.

They could even be called political enemies. But the young vice president had always been treated fairly by the Speaker, and he acknowledged Rayburn's greatness by having his signature engraved with all the others on a large silver tray that was presented to Mr. Sam.

But 1959 was not entirely a year of celebrations for the Speaker. After his trip to the Fourth District during the Easter recess, Rayburn realized that the country was entering a rather serious economic recession. One measure Rayburn sought to have passed by Congress was the Housing bill. If passed, this bill would put 260,000 Americans to work who were unemployed at the time. But the Rules Committee of the House had not reported the bill out of the Committee for consideration. It was deadlocked in a six to six tie vote because two of the Democrats were voting with the four Republicans to keep the bill from reaching the floor for debate. On his return from the Easter recess, Rayburn told the chairman of the committee, Howard Smith, that he would bypass the committee if they did not break the tie and bring the bill up for consideration. It would be difficult, Rayburn knew, but he was confident he had enough votes behind him to get the bill before the House. The Rules Committee is so powerful, it has often been called the "third house of Congress." Only through the use of a few complicated House regulations can a bill be debated and voted upon without first having the approval of the Rules Committee. And even then, the bill usually must be debated and voted on in a single day!

Rayburn explained to both the Democrats and Republicans on the Committee that the general welfare of the nation was at stake, and that this was no time to be playing politics. Two members finally agreed, and the Housing bill was brought out of the committee for action, and another Rayburn victory.

Mr. Sam and his favorite horse, Whistlestop

Mr. Sam ready to ride out over his ranch.

[172]

A cold drink
from the well

Lining up
a balky constituent
at milking time

Mr. Sam
relaxed in
his ranch cabin

[173]

The 86th Congress ended its first session in August and the Speaker spent much of the remaining months in the large Rayburn home west of Bonham. For Rayburn, these were the happiest times of all. In Congress he worked hard and had the reward of knowing he was doing a good job. But the quiet days in the old family home and on the ranch he loved were the happiest of all. These were the times in which Mr. Sam could visit with his family and with his friends. They were also days in which he could plan for the coming national election of 1960. For at 77, the man from Fannin County continued to look to the future.

The second session of the 86th Congress opened on Sam Rayburn's 78th birthday, January 6, 1960. Soon after the first day's activities, Washington newspapermen sought him out in his Capitol office. It was an election year, and no one in Washington was more an authority than the Fourth District's Mr. Sam.

When he was asked one important question, Rayburn said, "Well, he's my candidate." The subject was Rayburn's friend, Senate Majority Leader Lyndon B. Johnson. The tall Senator had been mentioned as a possible Presidential candidate in 1956 when he was the Texas delegation's "favorite son" choice. When the time came to choose a vice presidential nominee, both Johnson and a young Massachusetts senator named John Kennedy ran close behind the eventual winner, Senator Estes Kefauver of Tennessee. It now appeared that Johnson might be a strong contender for the Presidential nomination.

As 1960 began, the Democratic Party had many possible candidates. In addition to Lyndon Johnson, many of the liberal Democrats still wanted to see Adlai E. Stevenson given another chance at the White House. Kefauver obviously wanted the nomination. So did Averill Harriman of New York. And Stuart Symington, Senator from Missouri. Another candidate was the young politician from Massachusetts, John F. Kennedy. Ever since the end of the 1956 convention, Senator Kennedy had been working carefully to build himself into a contender for the Presidential nomination. While Johnson had the powerful backing of Sam Rayburn, Stevenson had the liberals, Harriman the powerful machine of Tammany Hall in New York, and Symington the recommendation of former President Truman—Kennedy had only his overpowering desire. All of the candidates had sufficient financing to back their efforts; so it became a matter of whose plan was really the most effective. In taking his candidacy direct to the people, without relying on the influence of others, Jack Kennedy was taking the lead that had been set years ago by Sam Rayburn himself. One was a poor farm boy from Texas, the other a wealthy Bostonian; but both knew the secret of winning over the voters of the nation.

On January 11, Sam Rayburn made an announcement that indicated he was planning to take an active part in the coming Presidential nomination. He informed the press he would not serve the convention as its permanent chairman. "I have a great desire to see one convention from the floor," Rayburn said in explanation. It was not necessary for him to add that he could do much more to help Lyndon Johnson from the floor than he could as the permanent chairman.

A few days later, the 78-year-old Speaker made another announcement that surprised a few of his friends. Some people thought Rayburn was ready to retire from Congress with the completion of his 24th consecutive term in the House of Representatives. They were wrong. The man from Fannin County wrote his check in payment of his filing fee and mailed it to

Bonham. Rayburn was seeking a 25th term in Congress! The only change all the years seemed to have made was in Mr. Sam's vision. He could no longer read for so long as he used to do. But otherwise his doctors pronounced him in excellent health and ready for a 25th term if that was his desire.

In 1960, almost every action of the famed Speaker was good for a story in the Washington papers. And when something special came along, it was usually printed in national magazines as well. An outstanding example of how Rayburn made good stories concerned a young newspaperman Rayburn knew only through his press conferences. The man had suffered a severe personal tragedy: his young daughter had died. The news saddened Mr. Sam when he heard of it. The morning after the youngster's death, Sam Rayburn got up early and went to the Washington apartment of the reporter, who was stunned when he answered the door and found the famous Speaker standing outside.

"I just came by to see what I could do to help," Mr. Sam said slowly.

Nervously, the young reporter assured the Speaker there was nothing to do—that all the arrangements were being made.

"Well, have you all had your coffee this morning?"

"No, we haven't had time."

"Well, I can at least make the coffee this morning."

With that, Sam Rayburn walked into the apartment and found his way to the kitchen. The shocked reporter watched Mr. Sam measuring out the coffee. Then he remembered from a press conference that Rayburn was to have met with President Eisenhower on this same morning.

"Mr. Speaker," the newspaperman said, "I thought you were supposed to be having breakfast at the White House this morning."

"Well," Rayburn replied, "I was, but I called the President and told him I had a friend who was in trouble, and I couldn't come."

It was as simple as that. This was Sam Rayburn. This was the man whose great power came most of all from the common touch. Greatness he carried lightly on his square shoulders; it never seemed to weigh him down.

The year 1960 rolled on into the spring toward the national conventions in the summer. Candidate Johnson managed to get away from his post as majority leader of the Senate long enough to make a speechmaking trip through the western states of Colorado, Utah, Nevada, and Wyoming. Rayburn helped by making a speech in Johnson's behalf at Richmond, Virginia. But it was difficult in the important spring months for Johnson and Rayburn to campaign all-out. There was simply too much of importance to be attended to in the Congress. The Summit Meeting between Eisenhower and Soviet Premier Nikita Khrushchev collapsed, and the two Democratic leaders were busy giving the Republican President the support of their party in both the Senate and the House. Meanwhile, candidate Jack Kennedy was busy lining up his delegates for the Democratic national convention.

At the state convention of the Democratic Party in Texas, Rayburn and Johnson were now fighting for control against the "liberal" wing of the party. Earlier, the two of them had successfully fought off the conservative extremists of the far "right." Now the far "left" was giving them trouble. But in the end, Rayburn again controlled the convention and was assured the Texas delegation would be solidly behind Senator Johnson. In total votes at the national convention, Rayburn felt fairly certain of having between 450 and 500 on the first ballot. It took 761 votes to win the nomination.

As the convention was about to begin, Rayburn commented on Johnson's strength. He knew Kennedy had run up an impressive record in the primary elections and that the young Massachusetts Senator was bringing a larger number of votes into the convention. Still, if Rayburn could get Johnson through the first roll call, Rayburn felt there was a good chance. He expressed regret that the majority leader of the Senate simply had not had enough time to wage an effective cross-country campaign such as Kennedy's. The man from Fannin County emphasized that he was not "against" Jack Kennedy, but that he was "for" Lyndon Johnson. As the convention began, it was clear that Lyndon Johnson alone had any chance at all to stop the well-run Kennedy organization. Sam Rayburn was known by all to have in his pocket more "political I.O.U.'s" than anyone in the nation—if he decided to start collecting.

Sam Rayburn nominated Lyndon Johnson on July 13, describing him as a man who belonged to "no class, no section, no faction—a man for all Americans. . . ." Later, as the roll

Lyndon Johnson watched Mr. Sam put him in nomination for the Presidency.

[178]

call started, the television cameras spent a great deal of time on the Speaker, shifting to him frequently as the state votes were announced. Rayburn sat quietly, realizing it would be a tremendous upset to stop the Kennedy machine at such a late date. After the roll call was finished, Kennedy held a huge lead over Johnson. And when Wyoming changed its 15 votes to Kennedy, the necessary 761 vote total was reached. John F. Kennedy became the Democratic Party's Presidential nominee.

The television camera flashed to the Texas delegation in time to catch disappointment—although not surprise—on the face of the Speaker of the House and honorary chairman of the convention. His remarks were short and to the point: "We fought a good fight. Of course we'll support Mr. Kennedy. That's the Democratic way—and I'm a Democrat." It was a typical statement from Mr. Democrat himself.

Going into the convention, Sam Rayburn had been of the opinion that Johnson should not accept the vice presidential nomination, even if it were offered him. He felt the majority leader was too valuable in the Senate. But shortly after Kennedy's nomination, the question of the second place on the ticket came up in all seriousness. Rayburn's advice to Johnson again was to turn down the offer.

Later, the Speaker returned to his hotel in Los Angeles with his assistant, John Holton. As soon as they entered Rayburn's room, the telephone rang. A discussion was being held concerning the vice presidency for Johnson, and Jack Kennedy wanted to talk about it with Sam Rayburn.

"Mr. Speaker," Kennedy said, "I want to talk to you about this."

"All right, I'll be glad to meet you at your room."

Kennedy said no, he would rather come to Rayburn's room. Mr. Sam agreed, and the nominee said he would be there within 20 minutes. Kennedy arrived late, for the liberals in the party were trying to convince him to choose some other candidate than Lyndon Johnson. When Kennedy entered Rayburn's room, the two men went immediately to a quiet corner, and the nominee began talking to the Speaker, trying to convince him that Johnson should accept the vice presidential nomination. Kennedy explained that the vice presidency would be more important than it had ever been before in his administration, and that Johnson would be far more valuable than he could ever be in the Senate.

Finally Rayburn brought the conversation to a climax as he asked Kennedy what Johnson's own desire was. Jack Kennedy told Rayburn that Johnson would not commit himself until the Speaker had indicated his own position in the matter. Rayburn paused, then told the young Presidential nominee that it was all right, that he was now convinced Lyndon Johnson should accept the vice presidential nomination. For all practical purposes, this sealed the decision.

At 8:30 the following morning, John F. Kennedy arrived at Lyndon Johnson's room to make the formal statement that Johnson was his choice for a running mate. Johnson paused briefly after Kennedy's statement, then shook the nominee's hand. "All right, Jack," the Senator said. "For the good of the country and the Party, I'll accept. You can count me in."

When the convention reopened to nominate the vice presidential candidate, the television cameras were again on the man from Fannin County. They caught this time the great happiness he felt as Lyndon Johnson swept to victory on the first ballot. Above him fluttered the Texas flag and around him his friends pressed to offer their congratulations. For Rayburn, the real victory was the new unity that had been found in the Democratic party.

[180]

Mr. Sam applauded Johnson's nomination for the vice presidency.

UNITED PRESS INTERNATIONAL

Kennedy's decision proved to be a wise one, for Lyndon Johnson held a wide appeal in both the South and the West. Texas, which had voted for Eisenhower in the two previous elections, was considered safe for the Democrats with Johnson on the ticket. Kennedy visited the major Texas cities during the national campaign; and when he moved into the Republican stronghold of Dallas, Mr. Sam was with him. He introduced the Democratic nominee to a capacity crowd in Dallas' huge Memorial Auditorium. As Mr. Sam spoke, catching and holding the thousands of persons there, it was difficult to believe that Dallas was a Republican city. Rayburn used a liberal sprinkling of Truman's "give 'em hell" tricks, reminding the audience that "those who got the richest under the Democrats now hate us the most!" The crowd alternately laughed and

[181]

cheered as Rayburn rambled on. A Republican onlooker in the audience was moved once to stand and cheer with the Democrats beside him. The man from Fannin simply could not be denied.

When the votes were counted in the November election, Texas once more was in the Democratic column. And throughout the South, Johnson's name pulled state after state to Kennedy. This—it turned out—was the Kennedy margin of victory. For among a total of 69,000,000 votes, Kennedy received only 112,800 more than Republican Richard M. Nixon.

In December, the Speaker of the House was invited to join in a major meeting with the President-elect at Palm Beach, Florida. After several sessions with Kennedy, Johnson and Mike Mansfield—who was to take Johnson's place as majority leader in the Senate—Rayburn restlessly began glancing out the window toward the inviting fishing area. Finally he decided to take his chances at catching a few little ones. Humorously, he told some newspapermen that he would catch the "big ones" in January when Congress opened. Mrs. Kennedy followed the Speaker along the pier and snapped a now-famous photograph of him as he threw his line into the water.

On the photograph, Mrs. Kennedy wrote: "The fish haven't got a chance! Affectionately—Jacqueline Kennedy." To this, Jack Kennedy added a note of his own—"And neither has the House of Representatives."

Chapter **20**

Back Home

T he 87th Congress convened on January 3, 1961, and went through the expected formality of electing Sam Rayburn of Texas as its Speaker. A few days later, it celebrated January 6 as the 79th birthday of its most distinguished member, now entering his eighth full term as Speaker and his 25th consecutive term in the House of Representatives. His was a career that had already become a national legend. For him to go down in history as the greatest Speaker of all required only one thing. He would have to avoid suffering a tragic defeat. At 79, if Rayburn were to weaken and lose an important legislative battle, he could easily meet the same fate as his good friend Joe Martin.

So it was a tremendous surprise when the news came out that the man from Fannin County was going to do just the opposite of following the safe route to national immortality. He announced his intention to break the stranglehold of the Rules Committee on the House of Representatives! If he won, his stature as the greatest speaker in history would rise to even greater heights. If he failed, it could mean the end of his political career. At 79, Sam Rayburn decided to put his tremendous prestige on the line in the greatest battle of his career.

Mr. Sam felt the Rules Committee could not be allowed to interfere with Kennedy's New Frontier program of legislation. He discussed the matter with Jack Kennedy and came to his hard decision. Meanwhile, plans were going forward for the January 20th inauguration of Kennedy and Johnson.

Early in the month, Mr. Sam was trying to solve the problem of finding the best way to end the Rules Committee's power to block legislation. The committee had 12 members, 4 Republicans and 8 Democrats. But two of the Democrats had been voting with the Republicans; and by continuing to do so, they were certain to keep the Kennedy program tied up permanently. The two Democrats were William Colmer of Mississippi and the Chairman, Howard Smith of Virginia.

On January 17, just three days before the inauguration, the Democrats of the House met in a caucus. The conservatives wanted to continue with the Rules Committee unchanged. The liberals wanted to eliminate Colmer's membership in it. Others wanted to enlarge the committee to break the conservative control of Smith, Colmer, and the four Republican members. To the caucus, Mr. Sam said: "I have received thousands of letters opposing this change in the Rules Committee. About eighty per cent of the letters, I might add, came from people who voted for Richard Nixon. Most of them believe in maintaining the status quo or in turning back the clock."

The next day Sam Rayburn announced that he favored expansion of the Rules Committee by three members—two Democrats and one Republican—which would break the six to six tie and bring the Administration's bills to the floor of the House by an eight to seven vote of the committee. Rayburn did not think it was fair to consider removing Colmer, who had opposed the Kennedy-Johnson ticket, for voting according to his beliefs.

There was, however, a brief delay on January 20, as John F. Kennedy was inaugurated President, along with Lyndon B. Johnson as vice president. It was a great day for Rayburn. The new east front of the Capitol was completed in time for the ceremony, and his close friend was being sworn into the second highest office in the executive branch of the government. Rayburn himself swore Johnson into office; and when the short ceremony was finished, he clasped Vice President Johnson's hand firmly in his own. "God bless you," Mr. Sam said.

Within a matter of days, Rayburn's great fight in the Congress was resumed. In the first days of Kennedy's administration, Sam Rayburn's stand became the hottest news story of the month. Newspapers ran daily accounts of his comments and the slow procedure that would ultimately lead to his grim battle on the floor of the House. His picture appeared on the cover of *Time* after he risked the prestige of his career.

January 26 had been set as the date for the expansion measure to come before the House. The Rules Committee voted the question out for debate on January 24, and everything seemed to be in order. It would be a battle between the liberal and conservative elements of the House. Many Republicans, such as Joe Martin, could be counted on to help Rayburn. But, at the same time, many Southern Democrats would oppose him.

In a surprise move on January 25, the Speaker announced that the vote had been postponed until January 31. He explained that several members of the House were ill and that the bad winter weather was causing severe transportation problems. He felt he was a little out in front, perhaps by three votes. He said: "I don't think we will be in worse shape Tuesday than we would be tomorrow and I think we'll win."

[185]

On January 31, the vote came just as Rayburn had announced. And the great Speaker waited carefully as the roll of the membership was called. At the end, 212 members of the House had voted to keep the old membership of the Rules Committee without additions. But, for the Rayburn column, 217 voted "aye"! It was the greatest victory for the Speaker since his extension of the Selective Service Act before World War II. Once again, the Rayburn gavel came down hard, smashing into defeat the members who had challenged him. At 79, his was still the most powerful voice in the halls of Congress! "We won and I am satisfied," was his only remark.

As Easter of 1961 approached, Rayburn decided to make the long trip home to Bonham. The Congress had done well since the expansion of the Rules Committee, and Mr. Sam was ready for a rest at the quiet old home west of town. While he was there, he made several pointed comments on the recent election to fill Lyndon Johnson's vacant Senate seat. The Democratic candidate had been William Blakley, a conservative Dallas millionaire; the Republican had been John Tower, an extreme conservative in the old Texas Regular tradition. As it turned out, the moderate and liberal Democrats of the state did not really have a candidate to vote for in the election. The only apparent difference between Tower and Blakley was that Tower was short and Blakley tall. So the Democrats simply did not bother to vote. With over 2,000,000 registered voters, only half of them cast their ballots in the election. In Rayburn's view, a true Democrat would have won. Meanwhile, the Republicans were bragging that Texas had at last become a two-party state. They looked forward eagerly to the election of other Republican candidates in the future. Rayburn's comment proved historic: "If the Republicans think they have achieved a two-party system in Texas, let them try to elect a governor!"

In the following year, the Republicans did try. Democrat John Connally, a close friend of Rayburn and Johnson, who had served as Kennedy's Secretary of the Navy, beat the Republican candidate easily. Mr. Sam's prediction was correct as usual.

In the summer, more honors came to the great Speaker. John McCormack of Massachusetts introduced a resolution on June 12, 1961: "Resolved, That the House of Representatives hereby extends its heartiest congratulations to its beloved Speaker, the Honorable Sam Rayburn, who, today, has served in the high office of Speaker of the House of Representatives for 16 years, 273 days—more than twice as long as any other Speaker in the history of the United States. . . ." No longer was it enough for Rayburn to set new records—he was now doubling them! The only records to be broken were Mr. Sam's.

From the White House, President Kennedy wrote: "It gives me great pleasure to offer my congratulations today when the length of your service as Speaker has doubled that of an earlier Member, Henry Clay. . . . immeasurable is the respect, esteem, and affection which all of us who have served with you hold for you today. With warmest regards and best wishes, sincerely, John F. Kennedy."

The indestructible Speaker took it all in stride. He turned his attention to helping the World War I hero, Sergeant York, in settling his burdensome income tax debt to the government. To Mr. Sam's mind, the nation was also indebted to York— and he saw to it that arrangements were made to reduce the $172,000 tax bill to only $25,000. Rayburn then started a fund with his own personal donation of $1,000. A few days later, Sergeant York's tax bill was marked paid in full.

But with the full heat of the Washington summer, the 79-year-old Speaker seemed to tire. Still, he remained in the great chair on the high rostrum of the House as he had for more

[187]

years than many Congressmen could remember. But the indestructible was now beginning to weaken. As fate was to dis-
cover, it would not be an easy victory. The man from Fannin
County slowly lost his appetite in the long hot summer days
and his weight went down slightly for the first time since he had
been in the nation's Capitol. He worked on anyway, presiding
over the House he loved.

Toward the end of the summer, however, the Speaker
was feeling even worse. No longer did he have the energy that
had been his for 79 and a half years. Tired, he also began to
suffer from an annoying ache in his back. At last—and very
reluctantly—the Speaker agreed to a medical examination. Mr.
Sam's opinion was that he was suffering from an old-fashioned
case of lumbago. Apparently he was as convincing with the
Washington doctors as he was in Congress, for they agreed.

Rayburn returned to the Speaker's chair in the House, be-
ginning again his daily routine. But the backache grew worse.
Finally, he called his Bonham physician, Dr. Joe Risser, and
made plans to go home for a while until he was feeling better.
He announced his plans in a short and dramatic statement: "I
want to die with my boots on and with my gavel in my hand.
They are going to have to carry me out of here, God willing.
I love this House."

On August 31, 1961, Sam Rayburn returned home. He
visited Dr. Risser's modern Bonham hospital each day. And
Dr. Risser sent word to the White House daily to keep Kennedy
and Johnson informed of the Speaker's progress. Through the
early days of September, the examinations continued, and Rayburn had the usual flood of visitors in his big, comfortable
home. One of those, a Dallas photographer, Shel Hershorn, Rayburn greeted with his usual warmth. He told Hershorn he would
be happy to have some pictures made a little later on when he

was feeling better and had got his appetite back.

The examinations by Dr. Risser continued throughout September, until the doctor decided his patient should go to Baylor Medical Center in Dallas. Still not feeling any better, the Speaker gave his consent. On October 2, the Dallas newspapers carried stories of their distinguished visitor from Bonham. Rayburn walked into the huge white hospital and immediately began a series of what he described as "poking and prodding" tests. A few days later, October 5, 1961, the announcement was made by Dr. Robert F. Short, Jr. The Speaker of the House of Representatives was ill with incurable cancer.

The government of the United States was stunned. President Kennedy asked the nation to join his family in prayer for the great Speaker. Throughout Texas, eyes were moist as they had not been for a politician since the death of Franklin Roosevelt. It was a blow that struck at the very soul of the state.

The following day, Vice President Lyndon Johnson was at his friend's bedside in Baylor Medical Center. Within two days, the President's huge jet touched down at Dallas' Love Field. It was not an official visit to Dallas, and President Kennedy did not bother with the usual welcoming committees. He went straight to Sam Rayburn's sickroom. As he brushed by the newspapermen, the President's face was tight and serious. As he left the hospital, he was obviously moved by his visit with the Speaker. Kennedy's voice was taut as he delivered a brief statement: "He's sick of course. I was glad I could be with him. He was in good spirits and showed enough courage for anybody." For Mr. Sam, that much could be counted on!

Former President Truman arrived in Dallas within another few days and spent about five minutes with Mr. Sam. For Truman, it was a great blow to see his great friend so ill. But Rayburn was fighting hard—and this the fighter Truman admired. It was a trait they had shared in Washington.

At last, toward the end of October, it was announced that the Speaker would return to the Joe Risser Hospital in Bonham on October 31. Everything had been done that was possible at Baylor, and Mr. Sam expressed an earnest desire to be at home in the Fourth District, his beloved "native heath." As November began, Mr. Sam was at home once more.

During the next few days, the reports from Bonham were pretty much the same. Rayburn at times felt better and even made a few jokes. Then, he was worse and at last he got no better. On Thursday, November 16, 1961, the Speaker of the House of Representatives died. One of the great men of the Republic became an important part of the nation's history.

But Mr. Sam's death did not end the story. A few days later, the small town of Bonham was visited by the greatest rush of prominent men the state of Texas has ever seen. They came not to Dallas or to Houston, for nothing in these places was of such importance. They came to Bonham—105 members of the Congress, former President Truman, former President Eisenhower, President Kennedy and Vice President Johnson, Supreme Court Justice Tom Clark, a score of Texas officials along with 15,000 of Sam Rayburn's friends of the Fourth District—all to pay final respect.

The funeral was held on Saturday, November 18, and was telecast from Bonham throughout the United States. A simultaneous service was held in the House Rayburn loved in Washington; and the Chicago Symphony Orchestra provided music for the television audience. Among those watching, doubtless, was old Cactus Jack Garner, a former vice president who was unable now to leave his Uvalde home. When at last it was over and Mr. Sam was buried in Willow Wild Cemetery, there was a great emptiness in the nation. But the words

[190]

At Mr. Sam's grave, former Presidents Truman and Eisenhower, President Kennedy, House Parlimentarian Clarence Cannon, and Vice President Johnson were among the mourners.

of Mr. Sam himself came back to comfort those who grieved his death. "The wheels of this great body," Mr. Sam had said many times of the House, "the greatest institution ever conceived by man, must turn and move forward."

They did and the nation did. But it has not yet forgotten Mr. Sam of the Fourth District of Texas. Already, two memorials honor him. One, a powerful atomic submarine that bears his name. The other is simpler—and would have been more to Mr. Sam's own taste. The main street of Bonham has had new paint applied to its signposts in as bright a blue as the Texas sky. They read: Sam Rayburn Avenue.

Other honors are sure to come, for greatness such as Rayburn's can never die.